D0365010

Slithery Snakes
and Other Aids
to Children's Writing

Slithery Snakes and Other Aids to Children's Writing

Walter T. Petty
State University of New York at Buffalo

Mary Bowen

PRENTICE-HALL, INC., *Englewood Cliffs, New Jersey*

©1967
by PRENTICE-HALL, Inc.,
Englewood Cliffs, New Jersey

All rights reserved. No part of this book
may be reproduced in any form or by any means,
without permission in writing from the publisher.

Printed in the United States of America

ISBN: 0-13-813097-3

Library of Congress Catalog Card Number: 67-14574

10 9 8 7 6 5 4

PRENTICE-HALL INTERNATIONAL, INC., *London*
PRENTICE-HALL OF AUSTRALIA, PTY. LTD., *Sydney*
PRENTICE-HALL OF CANADA, LTD., *Toronto*
PRENTICE-HALL OF INDIA PRIVATE LIMITED, *New Delhi*
PRENTICE-HALL OF JAPAN, INC., *Tokyo*

Preface

This book is based upon a very simple concept, the conviction that children can and should be taught many of the aspects of creative writing heretofore largely reserved for those adults preparing to become professional writers. Although we have tested with at least some degree of success all of the suggestions we have to offer, we feel that many of them are brand new and have not before been offered to teachers who want to help children learn to write. Although you may be skeptical, we hope very much that you will read further and give us a chance to prove our point.

Ideas are transient and not exclusively possessed. We acknowledge that the ideas here came from many persons, particularly our teacher and pupil friends over the years. We thank all of them for helping us and, we hope, for helping you.

Special appreciation is due Barbara Herberholtz for bibliography suggestions and Jean Schmidt for typing and serving as a "sounding board." We also appreciate the encouragement from Clem and Bob.

W.T.P.
M.B.

Contents

**Slithery Snakes
and Other Aids
to Children's Writing**

Once upon a time there was a slithery snake on a muddy hill. He was on top. He went slithering and sliding in the slooshy, sloshy, sticky, gooey mud. He slithered and slooshed and slid all the way to the bottom! (Chapter 5, page 68)

Creative Writing: Why Bother?

In today's world creativity is not just a nice thing to have. It is a grave necessity.

Edgar Dale

You probably picked up this book because you are interested in children and especially because you want to help them do more and/or better creative writing. Perhaps your motivation was not that directly related to the writing problems of the children you teach or will be teaching. At any rate, we're glad you looked because we think children's writing is important, and we have included many things here which we believe will help you in teaching children to write better.

We'll set forth some ideas for getting writing started and suggest how you may work with the building blocks and tools of the writer's trade useful to children. First, though, we want to discuss creative writing: what it is, what can be done about teaching it, and how it relates to all writing and other activities of children. The reason for this, of course, is that we believe that teaching action must be built upon a foundation. This foundation must be considered first.

1

What Is Creativity?

For one thing, it is right now a magic word. Everybody is interested in it—in defining, recognizing, developing, and utilizing it. Nationwide, we are demanding creative thinkers in all areas of science. We search for creative teachers. People even speak of the creative businessman. It seems that suddenly we have come to realize that the progress of civilization depends (as it really always has) upon new solutions, upon imagination and new ideas, upon the creativity of its people.

Still, what is creativity? Creativity occurs whenever isolated experiences and ideas are put into new combinations or patterns. It occurs as someone produces a new construction out of existing materials. The urge to create is in all of us. We do not have it in equal amounts or with equal inclination in every area of human concern. But it is there, and it helps us to live our lives to the fullest, whether we are decorating a cake, raising money for a church function, or entering a limerick contest. We do not have to be perched on a scaffold beneath the ceiling of the Sistine Chapel to qualify as creative.

As a child a person is often at his creative peak; he acts more instinctively, more intuitively, more spontaneously than he acts as an adult. Children, much more than adults, have the ability to perceive things each time anew. Preconceptions, imposed generalizations and perceptions, and the dulling habits which accrue to adulthood do not inhibit their expression of what their senses tell them. A view of the ocean, a bite of chocolate candy, a fuzzy teddy bear, a ride on a roller coaster—all are much more likely to be described with uniqueness and originality by a child.

Creativity, however, is an uncertain, risky, and sometimes even threatening aspect of human conduct. It tends to be repressed and controlled as a child becomes an adult—as, indeed, much of it needs to be if parents, teachers, and others of us are to survive. Yet at the same time, we feel compelled to do all we can to set up a wildlife preserve, as it were, for all the better aspects of a child's creativity, so that such aspects can have a place to be safe and allowed to grow. We adults seem to know instinctively that creativity must not be entirely hidden, and some of us know that too much hiding and suppression may have already occurred and want to prevent more from happening.

What Is Creative Writing?

Surely this question has caused at least as much controversy in some circles of educators as any in the language arts. Many teachers, however, especially those facing rows of expectant children each day, have been little concerned about answering it; they have worried little about a definition which will satisfy their literal-minded counterparts and the educators who write and talk about such things. Rather, they have been a great deal more concerned with having children write. We are inclined to hold with these practicing teachers and want all to get on with the business of teaching children to write better. As Robert Frost once said, poetry is "just taking the same old words and putting them together in a new way to say something you've been thinking about." We think this is pretty close to the essence of creative writing.

Professor Ruth K. Carlson, who intensively studied several thousands of children's stories, has reported seventeen qualities of what she calls *original* rather than *creative* writing.[1] The qualities she found are the following: (1) novelty or freshness; (2) individuality; (3) a personal quality revealing the self; (4) emotion or feeling; (5) "becomingness" related to identification; (6) imagination; (7) a recombination or restructuring quality; (8) an abstractive element consisting of finding the essence; (9) immediacy; (10) dynamic vitality; (11) curiosity; (12) reservoir of experiential data; (13) perceptive sensitivity; (14) flexibility or versatility; (15) symbolism; (16) coherent unity; and (17) an expressive-communicative element.

Such a listing may appear formidable, if one thinks that one needs to look for all these qualities in the writing of the children

[1] Ruth K. Carlson, "Seventeen Qualities of Original Writing," *Elementary English*, Vol. 38 (December, 1961), 576-579.

in one's class. This, however, was not Professor Carlson's point. She was seeking in the analysis the qualities that children put into their stories and she has summarized them by defining original writing as writing that is "individual, novel, or unusual." We think this also expresses well the essence of creative writing.

We go further than considering creative writing as occurring only in poetry or stories and hold the view that creative writing may have further utility and purpose. Surely utilitarian writing may take "the same old words and put them together in a new way to say something one has been thinking about." Surely, too, utilitarian writing may be "individual, novel, or unusual." We think, in fact, that any writing may have these qualities and be truly imaginative and spontaneous. We think, also, that it may be deliberate, factual, and written only after careful consideration. For example, a letter may be so written that the imagination is used, the senses are stimulated, and an artistic word-picture is painted for the reader. This is creativity; it is also practical and quite effective communication. Another letter might be just as practical, and possibly as communicative of basic thought, and yet lack the sparkle of creativity. Both represent "practical writing," but one shows creativity in a real sense and the other does not.

Thus creative writing may take many forms. A poem is usually a creative product, but so may be a story, a play, a report, the minutes of a meeting, or even an announcement about a lost article. It may have the utility needed to seek recovery of that lost article, or it may be as lacking in utility as a note in a personal diary. It may be a stanza jotted down hurriedly, or it may be prose produced after many hours of deep thought, self-editing, and polishing. In each case, however, if the writing is truly the individual's, if it shows a flash of something beyond the commonplace, it is creative.

Can Creative Writing Be Taught?

We say that it really *can* be taught—just as the other creative arts are—but it must be *taught*. While it is true that some painters, musicians, or dancers are innately talented and have received little teaching, the majority of persons engaged in these arts, professionally or simply for enjoyment, have received instruction—they have been *taught*.

> Let the wind push me, I don't care,
> As long as I need not pay a fare.
> Let it carry me over hill and dale;
> Let it carry me through fog and hail.
> Let the wind push me, I don't care,
> I like to feel it blow through my hair.
>
> *Kathleen S.*
> Grade 6
> Southwestern Central

While it is generally agreed today that one learns to write by writing, this is not a complete solution. Few teachers any longer believe that children may be taught to write simply by learning to identify parts of speech and by completing punctuation and usage exercises in workbooks (though many parents believe that these activities are the keys to good writing). This change in teachers' beliefs is all to the good, but simply having children write is not the sole answer either. Each written product could be no better nor no worse than the preceding product, if one held strictly to the idea that one learns to write by writing. More is needed, which is what this book is about.

We know that writing is a difficult task; we know that it is a task that is often frustrating. In writing, one must combine the ability to think, talk, spell, punctuate, and make sentences. And for the beginner the motor-mental act of directing the pencil is a major difficulty. There is no easy way. All of these things and more must be done. To write well, all must be learned.

Oral language comes first, with the quality of the later writing closely paralleling the quality of the speech. Factors which foster good oral expression also foster good and creative written expression. This we know, but we must hold on to it and keep it ever in mind. Motivation to write is basic, as is, equally, actually having something to say. Students must write because they want to—either for the joy of it or because it is necessary to their lives. They will not truly write unless there is something for them to say.

Creative Writing and Basic Writing Skills

Instruction in the skills necessary to good sentence construction and to clarity, unity, and effective organization of a composition is best given as the need arises. That is, as a child writes something he thinks is important and that he wants to do well, he is most interested in learning those skills which will make this writing meet the standards he seeks.

Creative writing, as writing which has the pupil's own personality, thoughts, and feelings in it, is the ideal medium for the teaching of writing skills. This should not mean that a child will be stopped in the middle of a sentence to insert punctuation or to determine whether or not his statement is a "run-on sentence." It does mean that through encouraging him to proofread, through helping him determine if his meaning is clear, through showing him how to change the order of words in a sentence, and so on, a teacher can functionally teach writing skills and still refrain from suppressing spontaneity and originality of expression.

The teacher who insists upon giving the mechanics of writing priority over the content and spontaneity of what the child has written is doomed to failure in his long-range goal of helping that child to become a better writer.

Further Values of Creative Writing

The teaching of creative writing brings rewards far beyond the teaching of basic writing skills. Though there are several other such rewards, we think the most valuable is that children engaged in creative writing are likely to be using more of their mental capabilities than they do for many other kinds of school activities. They are using their minds in "high gear," rather than dawdling along, as so many children do through much of the school day, with their mental engines idling. Minds in high gear are learning, are giving their best, and are providing the child with personal emotional satisfaction. For a child to feel himself creating something—intent on expressing his idea, and with the desire to do his best—is one of the finest and most enduring joys he will ever know.

There are other bonuses from creative writing but we have just given the one most people would consider of greatest importance. In the parlance of high-pressure salesmanship, we have "taken the customer to see the view from the top of the mountain," and surely fostering in a student the practice of using the mind to its capacity should be every teacher's topmost concern. It is anticlimactic to come back down, but there are other things to be said. Creative writing has other values.

In a sense, creative writing is therapeutic. Through the provision of satisfaction it may serve as a safety valve to bottled-up tensions. Feelings and thoughts close to a child's heart may be brought to the surface and released. Often a teacher gets an insight into a child's personality through this release, if it is genuinely spontaneous and original, truly creative. Of course, a teacher should never infringe on the privacy of a child by revealing to others things he has entrusted to her.

Creative writing, when done by all pupils in a class, also has the virtue of cutting across ability levels. Each child has some ability to express himself in words, and while the entire class is engaged in basically the same thing, each child is working at his own exact level of ability.

And there are still more values. Vocabulary is considerably developed as ideas are expressed and exchanged and new words used. Much incidental learning of "subject matter" takes place, too. Creative writing also causes children to be more observant, to note and think about events and about their environment. Creative writing helps to develop the self-discipline that everyone needs; discipline is a requirement of effective writing, as it is in any activity that has a purpose. And, unlike music or art or many other fields more conventionally associated with creativity, writing is downright inexpensive. And finally, it is fun—which may be simply another way to express what we were saying at the beginning of this section of the book.

Before You Start

If it is sincere and straightforward, if it is new and fresh . . . it is original in quality, even if others have made the same discovery.

John Dewey

Creative writing is not something that should be done only at a certain time on Friday afternoon! If this is "the time" for creative writing it is fairly certain that the classroom climate is directed primarily at "everything in its place" rather than at creativity. How do you view the question of *when* creative writing should be done? If you favor keeping things scheduled—and certainly there is great virtue in orderliness—you may need to think about the child's school environment, about the climate of your classroom, and about the role of climate in creativity. If you are inclined to let things come as they may—and again, there is virtue in dealing with happenings as they occur—you may also need to think about the environment, the climate and conditions, and their effects upon creativity. In fact, most teachers need to think about these things or at least review them.

You may wish, for example, to ask yourself questions such as these:

1. How long has it been since I have tried something in my classroom which I have never done before?
2. What ideas might I try and evaluate in order to provide motivation for myself and for the children?
3. Do I consider creativity as something to be taught, or as an approach to all things I teach?
4. What sort of classroom environment could I describe which would be most hostile toward children's creativity? Which elements of such an environment are present in my own classroom?
5. What is the minimum number of arbitrary rules and regulations necessary to keep order in my classroom?
6. Of the rules and regulations in my classroom and in my school which are not officially written down but exist only on a basis of it's-always-been-done-this-way, how many are truly necessary or even real?

This chapter is about the components of a good climate and the relationship between climate and creative writing.

The Teacher's Personality

The most important aspects of classroom environment are the teacher's personality and attitude. The personality and attitude which make up a good teacher *per se* make for a good teacher of creative writing. In general, the good teacher is not rigid. He is respectful of a child's personality and ways of doing things, is patient, and praises whenever honestly possible. An interesting person himself, he is also interested in all sorts of things and ideas and has an awareness (to some degree at least) of the world about him—an awareness that is inherent in children. He toys with ideas, relationships, and materials, and encourages children to do the same. He is relaxed, friendly, honest, and reasonable, and not afraid to be himself before a class. Finally, the good teacher seeks to bring order, logic, and sequence to the classroom to provide a counterbalance for the conglomeration of experiences and profusion of ideas which surround children today.

A good teacher tempers his enthusiasm for language and expression with consideration for the verbal reticence of some of his charges. He must stimulate, bring to mind, help put into words; yet more often he must be receptive, drawing out the ideas children possess, expecting without expecting too much.

In addition, a good teacher of writing is a good manager of time. He takes advantage of spontaneous situations as they arise, but also gives children an opportunity to reflect and absorb. He looks for opportunities for writing, and *plans* to have adequate time to go over children's work. Lastly, he has the courage to blaze a trail in departing from the staid, too-routine and uninspiring, textbook-guided daily path, secure in the knowledge of his competence.

There are a few things a good teacher of writing should not do. He should not seek and use the children's writing output to enhance his own status. Sincere appreciation of a piece of writing may be shared with others on the school staff but only because it is sincerely appreciated and merits commendation to the author. There should be no danger of intimate ideas shared in confidence being circulated in a way which might embarrass the writer.

The teacher who writes well himself—and all should try—should be thankful, but should not use the writing opportunities always to produce a "masterpiece" himself. Too, children are not fooled by deviousness: when a teacher has a good idea he should simply share it with the children, rather than attempting to maneuver it into their heads.

As far as more specific traits go, the single most important thing for a teacher of writing to have is a broad knowledge of the various skills of authorship, plus a considerable store of ideas for helping children along. To help teachers know more about writing is the major purpose of this book, which discusses the various skills of writing and offers a "smorgasbord" of specific teaching suggestions.

Input

Children are not going to write much unless they have something worthwhile to write about. The process of acquiring something to write about is called "input." Teachers can add to (but not subtract from!) the multitude of ideas children bring with them to school. The variety of things a teacher can do to add ideas is almost infinite: he can read to children, give them time to observe, appreciate, and talk about things (perhaps through dramatic play), give them books in profusion and an opportunity to read them. He can give attention to expressive words and apt phrases and how they may be used, and present concrete materials—objects, pictures, and sounds. Most of all, children can be urged to capitalize on their own real experiences, in and out of school.

A great deal of "input" can be brought into focus for each writing project. If the class is to write, for instance, a story about a chimpanzee, the children can be encouraged to recall a wide variety of information. They may remember a school trip to the zoo made last year, or a family visit during the summer. Many undoubtedly watched Tarzan or *Daktari* programs on television. Have any read books which included information on chimpanzees, or ever known anyone who had a chimp or a monkey for a pet? Have children seen any at a circus? (Also, how many children would be willing to visit the public library after school for additional chimpanzee research?)

The input of ideas and experiences should be nearly continuous. (You can't "fill up" a child with experiences the first six weeks of class and then spend the rest of the year drawing on the supply!) Input, in general, must continue throughout the year in the children's reading and through the on-going activities of the classroom: the children's work in social studies, science, health, music, and so on.

Just about all effective writing projects are started with a specific "dose" of input. Perhaps the class has been on a trip together, seen a film, examined objects brought to class, or simply discussed good descriptive phrases for a mood, a place, or an action. Specific input can even take the form of appreciating a good piece of writing. Even as the writing project gets under way, the input process should continue. The teacher can ask various children to tell or read aloud opening sentences and particularly good descriptive phrases, and can urge them to discuss ways in which the subject being described can be compared or contrasted with something else or otherwise share ideas which might spark others in the class. The "input" experience can sometimes be resampled by posting photos taken by the teacher or the children during a trip to an historic site if the children are writing about an event which took place there. Related materials can be provided, such as illustrations of field mice and their natural habitat for reference, if the class is attempting "The Adventures of a Field Mouse."

Finally, it is necessary to do more than give children opportunities for experience, even though these may be directly intended as a specific dose of input. Most children must be encouraged to be observant, to see how the spider web seen on the trip was put together—or even to see the web. They must be taught to give pause to the daily hardships of existence of the Eskimos seen in the film or to appreciate the craftsmanship of an Indian arrow. Some children may see, hear, taste, and feel things and yet gain only vague impressions and ideas, and perhaps none that are particularly imaginative, vivid, or beyond the commonplace. Input given for a specific writing project must be done prudently, must whet the children's interest, and must spark their creative spirits.

Opportunities for Writing

With each passing year it seems that subject matter requirements at each grade level increase. Yet no diminishing of attention to writing has been suggested. How, then, can time be found for creative writing projects? That the children who have the most time for writing are found in the classes of teachers who care the most for writing seems to be a truism. Teachers who want their children to write always manage to find some way to make time for it.

You have the problem of finding something to write about and you also have the problem of finding time in which to write. Put your problems to work—let one solve the other. Good teachers have long combined writing projects, for example, with social studies, assigning such things as an adventure story set in another land, a pioneer's diary, a description of how the baker bakes bread, and so on. This approach can be used just as well in connection with any subject matter. There is the traditional assignment in primary grades of having the children compose a story to accompany a picture they have drawn. Perhaps you can come up with new and more interesting variations. If your fifth grade class is studying weather in science, why not have them prepare a weather report in writing to be posted outside the classroom? Or let one group consult the style used in the local newspaper for the weather report, and write a report in the same style. Or, perhaps a group of more capable children would like to observe the manner in which the local television station presents the weather, and write a script for their own report. If your school has a physical fitness program involving the children in calisthenics, why not have the class compose rhymes to chant as the exercises are done?

There is another sort of thing you can do, although it may take a little courage at first. Simply abandon some of your Maginot Line thinking, if you're guilty of it. Time for writing can frequently be found by eliminating from the language arts period routine work not necessary for your particular group. You really do not need to try to defend and preserve every activity listed in a textbook or a curriculum guide, or even those that you did last year. You are a professional person, so make your own professional decisions. Give diagnostic tests to determine which work the children may omit, particularly which things may be omitted for specific children. In other words, individualize your instruction: take into account the genuine needs of the children, and choose that which is useful in the textbooks and other materials provided you. It is a little work getting organized, but you'll save yourself countless hours of drudgery checking routine exercises and recording grades. And—just incidentally—the children will love you for it!

There are many ways to care for the individual writing and language needs of a class. Here are other examples of specific techniques and methods for individualizing instruction:

1. Tabulating errors which occur frequently in children's writing and then giving instructional attention only to these er-

rors. At one time you may tabulate one sort of error—punctuation, for example—and at another some other kind, such as poor paragraphing.

2. Keeping in a folder samples of a pupil's writing, appraising these from time to time for instructional needs.

3. Grouping children for instruction, relying upon the children in a small group to help one another with language needs. Grouping may be done on the basis of needs, interests, ability to help one another, and so forth, rather than simply on generalized "ability."

4. Having individual children practice proofreading and self-editing, and following this up with work on practice exercises needed to help them eliminate errors.

5. Reconsidering the grouping from time to time. Remain flexible enough to shift children in and out of groups as each situation requires.

Teachers who hesitate to depart from a page-by-page textbook routine and to individualize instruction are reminded that there is a respectable body of research to indicate that the best way to produce good language usage (including writing) is to have sufficient experience in having something to say and having a purpose for saying it. Drills are useful for teaching some language skills, particularly punctuation, but are not very helpful in teaching sentence construction, organization of thinking, and similar skills—the essence of good writing.

Still another way to free blocks of time for writing is by scheduling a "fine arts" period to include art, music, dancing, literature, and creative writing. A variation of this is to include some creative writing in the literature appreciation portion of the reading program. Children in later years of school are particularly called upon to write their reactions to literature; appropriate adaptation of this type of writing to the earlier grades is good, if interests of children and their audiences are kept in mind.

It should be remembered that an opportunity to write need not always include the entire class. Individual children or small groups may be excused from other assignments. Care should be taken, when a small group of children or an individual child is writing, that they are sufficiently well started. Also, be sure the children can work alone or will have access to you for help.

Christine

Christine is a girl. She is very nice for a friend! One day she was looking into the window and saw something. She was so surprised that she almost fainted. She saw a duplicate, just like her. She went out and greeted the other Christine. This Christine was mean. So if you ever see Christine, ask her if she is the right one!

Tina, age 10

My Dream

My dream is about a dog that I want. I want to have a ranch with horses, cows, and especially a dog that I want. It is a big German Shepherd. I've always wanted this special dog because I'm ten years old and I've never had but one dog in my whole life, so that is why I want a big German Shepherd.

Andy, age 9

Outlets for Writing

Put creativity to work; it will make time for itself. Often children write simply because they love to. Much of the time a little more fondness for writing will be discovered, however, if they know their finished work will be read and admired by others. Outlets for children's writing may include reading aloud (stories or interesting reports) to another group or grade. They may include letters of all sorts (written for a purpose and mailed), or a creative writing booklet for parents and friends or as a keepsake. Some children prefer to keep a personal writing notebook, while others might enjoy sharing by posting their free-time work with that of others in a Writer's Corner in the classroom. Outlets are found in the PTA news circular, in the local newspaper, in commercial youth magazines such as *Junior Scholastic* or *Jack and Jill,* or in the school newspaper. Also to be included among possible outlets for children's writing are plays written either by the group or by individuals, descriptions of classrooms, and so forth, to exchange with other classes; captions for pictures; and bulletin board and newspaper advertisements. Don't overlook the bulletin boards and displays in the principal's office and in the hall, as well as those in the classroom.

As children study and work on projects, they will have need to write, to make this writing appealing and creative, to tell what they've learned and what their thoughts are. Outlets for children's work will present themselves if you, the teacher, have faith in the existence of children's basic need to communicate and in the quality of their communications, and if you keep looking for logical ways in which this communication can be extended.

Getting Writing Started

How to tell students what to look for without telling them what to see is the dilemma of teaching . . .
Abercrombie

How can you actually get children started with a writing project? There are, no doubt, as many ways as there are teachers and children. The purpose of this chapter is to list just a few, in terms of very specific suggestions. If you are new to the business of helping children write, we would like to help you get started. It doesn't matter which idea you choose, or if you choose one of your own (maybe that's better), but the important thing is to start, to help children translate their experiences into expression. Each successive writing effort should come more easily —for both teacher and children.

There is much material in this chapter, more than any teacher can possibly use for initiating a beginning series of writing projects. Don't worry about that. Pick out three or four suggestions or however many you need to get started and use them right now. We hope you will then go on with other materials in this book and refer back to this chapter later for further ideas. Perhaps at that time you will want to use the suggestions we make here as springboards for ideas of your own which relate more closely to the unique situation and needs of your class.

Specific Topics

The most time-worn, and often the most unsuccessful, method for getting children to write is the assignment of a topic. The difficulty with this procedure in sparking genuinely creative expression is that the topics assigned may either be trite or simply lacking in appeal. The topics suggested here may be new for you, though they have been used by other teachers and have proven to have intrinsic interest for children.

If I Had $1,000 to Spend
What Mother Forgot
The Count-Down
He Hurried Too Fast
The Day My Pet Learned to Talk
A Space Man Comes to Visit
How I Feel in the Dark
What the Animals in the Zoo Don't Like
The Year Santa Claus (or the Easter Bunny, Jack Frost, etc.)
  Was Lazy
I Was a Pine Seed
The Earliest Thing I Remember in My Life
The Puppy Who Was Sad
Early in the Morning
Walking Home in the Rain
The Story of a Dime
The Fire Engine
If I Could Fly
My Pet When It Was Growing Up
What a Dinosaur Did One Day
The Most Beautiful Thing I Ever Saw
What I Think About Winter
What an Ant Might Think About
Adventures of a School Desk
What I Do First Thing in the Morning
A Surprise for My Family
The Hot, Hot Day
The Cat That Ran Away

The Happy Airplane
The Fairy Godmother Who Lost Her Wand
Why the Hen Was Sad
Leftover Turkey
What a Color Means to Me
Sounds I Hear at the Beginning or Ending of the Day
If I Could Join the Circus
Some Things That Would Happen If All the Clocks Stopped
   Working
The Hobo Who Decided to Go Home
If I Could Become Invisible at Will
If I Owned a Pig
What My Big Sister Thinks of My Little Brother
Sounds on a Black Night
I Interviewed a Famous Person
A Trip on a Raft
What I Would Do If I Knew I Would Be Blind in Three Days
Ten Years From Now
The Nicest Person I Know
Dear Santa Claus
All About Riding Horses
"Ouch!"
What I Think My Favorite TV Character Likes to Do
How I Feel About Walking Barefoot in the Mud
The Little Child Who Didn't Want to Grow Up
The Beach
All About Being Stubborn
My Favorite Pair of Shoes
If I Were Living Long Ago
An Ideal Place to Be
If I Were a Kite
The Robot Who Cried

Assigned Content

A variation of the assignment of a topic is the assigning of content for the writing. According to Alvina Burrows,[1] story

[1] Alvina T. Burrows, *What Research Says to the Teacher: Teaching Composition.* Washington: National Education Association, April, 1959.

content most popular with young writers includes "ghosts, goblins, and haunted houses; rugged pioneers, early American Indians, or other primitive peoples; space journeys and interplanetary explorations; tall tales and sojourns into the microscopically tiny; persons of superhuman strength or speed closely akin to that of many folk heroes; machines that come alive and talk or otherwise behave like human beings . . ." Human feelings and situations acted out by animals are also universally popular.

Of course, simply saying, "Write a story about ghosts," or even "We've been reading about pioneers. See if you can write a story about a pioneer," will often not bring forth much expression, let alone much creativity. Putting content in an appealing and thought-provoking framework will provide a better impetus for stirring creativeness and arousing expression.

Try one of these frameworks (or your own):

1. Halloween is the time for ghosts, goblins, and haunted houses; for jack-o'-lanterns, flickering lights, and spooky shadows; and for strange sounds, weird noises, and eerie silences. Take time to remember some exciting things which have happened to you on Halloween. See if you can write a Halloween story that will really make us think Halloween is right here. Try to make your writing vivid by including as many sights, sounds, smells, tastes, and feelings as possible.

A Witch

One day a witch started to pitch,
But she had to itch,
So she didn't pitch.
After she itched,
She started to pitch,
But she still had to itch,
So she never pitched.

Cathy, grade 4

2. Some Indians lived in wigwams, others in teepees, hogans, or longhouses. Some Indians made baskets; others made pottery or did craftwork in wood or leather. Can you write a story about one tribe of Indians and tell something about the actual lives of

the people? See if you can tell about just one hour of Indian life. Keep in mind the tribe, how they got their food, what kind of countryside they lived in (desert, pine forest, etc.), what their houses were like, their weapons, handicrafts, and customs.

3. One of the problems facing the first men who land on the moon is how they will move about, since gravity is much less there than on earth but also because we are not sure whether the moon's surface may be walked on. Write a story about a moon landing; pretend you are one of those landing. Keep in mind everything you know about the moon and space travel: things you have read in books or seen on television, what you have learned in science lessons.

Invented Circumstances

Invented circumstances also expand the assigned content idea further. Such circumstance invention lends itself exceedingly well to correlation with social studies and science activities but is not limited to them. The following list is intended merely to suggest possibilities which may be tailored to an individual teacher's classroom situation:

1. You are a manufacturer of toys for children and have just invented a new toy. Name it. Design the packaging. Write the advertising.
2. A group of men are talking about how each can best encourage people to conserve a natural resource. They are a poet, a playwright, a producer of animated cartoons, and a marionettist. What does each say?
3. You are among a group of people traveling from the eastern United States to California via the Isthmus of Panama during the gold rush. Keep a record of events as you make the journey from the Atlantic to the Pacific across Panama.
4. Pretend you are one of the firemen in your fire-fighting department. Pretend there is a fire near where you live. Tell what you do as you help to put out the fire.
5. You are among a group of "wildcatters" who search for oil

wells. Your team brings in a "gusher." Tell about what happened.

6. Each guest at the first Thanksgiving makes a speech. Pretend that you are an Indian, one of the Puritan ladies, or the Governor. Write what you would say.

7. You and your family are visiting in Mexico. Write a letter home telling a friend where you have been and what you have seen during the past three days. Don't forget to describe the weather and tell what the food is like; also tell about your means of transportation.

8. You are running. You are running very fast. Imagine why you are running (i.e., in a race, running from something you fear, etc.). Tell exactly how you feel emotionally and how you feel physically.

9. You are a famous explorer who has just made an important discovery. You are being interviewed on television. What does the interviewer ask you? What are your answers? What things will you be sure to mention if he doesn't ask about them?

10. Pretend you are the largest tree in your neighborhood. Tell about important events and the changes time has brought.

11. You are a scientist, working on a project in plant nutrition. You have planted a number of plants and are conducting an experiment showing what happens when they are not given certain elements. Keep a journal of your progress, day by day, telling what happens to the plants.

12. Pretend you are a statue, and that you know exactly what kind of statue you are. (General Grant on his horse in the park, a Roman statue in a museum, etc.) Come to life. What do you do?

13. Pretend you are an inanimate object (a parking meter, a little boy's socks, etc.). Make a list of your complaints.

14. You are a famous literary character (Huck Finn, Scrooge, etc.). Tell what you do on one particular morning.

15. You are a wild animal (beaver, zebra, etc.). Tell about your home, how you find food, and how you protect yourself.

16. Describe some common happening on earth as if you were an

observer from another planet seeing earthlings for the first time.

17. You are the pilot of a large transcontinental jet airliner which has just taken off from an airport. You notice one engine is on fire. Tell what happens next.

18. A fire engine has just screeched to a halt in front of the building across the street and you notice a thin line of smoke curling from an upstairs window. What has happened in the building?

19. You are lying on the bank of a stream watching your fishing line. Suddenly you hear a rustle in the leaves behind you. You jump up. Tell what happens next.

Nonsense Titles

Sometimes the suggestion of nonsensical titles will stimulate interesting stories and will appeal to children. Generally, too, they will lead to suggestions of such titles. Here are some to try:

The Day the Gleefle Schnoofed
Don't Forget the Trolofasts
All About Grandfather's Glim
The Cheerful Schnize
The Squigdee and the Wingbat
The Snolofu Who Wouldn't Smile
Little Joe Meets the Jimgimdee
A Journey to Cambolinee
Why the Wiggydose Will Never Forget Dillybump
In the Buckbrigs House
Three Miles From Nillypoo
Hagglesno and the Swagg
An Adventure in Pollygoop

All About Grandfather's Glim

Grandfather got a gorgeous glim from George Glimgiver. George got the glim from Gabooba who stole it from the glim shop.

A glim is a very popular thing. It whirls and twirls and then explodes.

A glim costs only eight moomas plus one mifit tax.

Greg, grade 6

The Cheerful Schnize

The cheerful Schnize was a jolly old fellow, except when he got mad. When he was happy he would go hippity skip down to the stream and sail his boat or go swimming. But when he was mad he shook his schnize house by his temper tantrums. Then he got a spank from his mother.

One day the Schnize thought he would go out for an adventure. He thought he would go camping, so he got his equipment and went camping. He thought he would go down by the stream in the woods. When he got there he set up his tent. When he went to bed that night he heard strange sounds. That really scared him. The only sounds he had really heard were an owl and a mouse.

What a silly Schnize!

Wendy, grade 6

Working From a Given Beginning

Working from a given beginning need not be as structured or as restricting to children as it might seem at first. Beginnings might range in length from a few words to an unfinished story which needs only the ending. Some beginnings predicate the nature of the ending with only minor variations, while others are merely a starter, leaving the topic wide open for the imagination of the writer.

These beginning sentences and phrases should suggest the range and scope of beginnings which may be used.

I was an acorn lying in the tall grass.
During Easter vacation I went to Catalina.
A clown is the nicest man to know.
I wish I could . . . .

It was the middle of the night and everyone in the house was asleep.

On the table were a shoelace and a red crayon.

Once upon a time, long, long ago . . . .

Jim, Bill, and Sue were walking to school.

I was frightened when I first saw that old house. The screen door was hanging part way open, and the setting sun cast slanting shadows across the weed-grown lawn.

I thought he was the meanest person I had ever known.

"I don't care what you say, I know I'm right," she said.

I just can't open this door!

The sun had barely risen, but already I could tell what kind of day this would be.

All the way home, I kept wondering how I was going to explain this to my parents.

The old crippled lion crept slowly through the tall grass.

Bulldozers began climbing the hill as the sun appeared over its top.

"She's gone! Now I am going to find her diary," muttered John as he crept up the stairs.

Bill stood stock still. His legs refused to move. The sweat broke out on his forehead.

There was a strange silence about the forest that night.

Waves rolled endlessly toward the shore, crashing thunderously against the gray rocks and sending countless sprays of foam skyward.

Beginnings of stories which go beyond a sentence or two may be used. Often these longer beginnings are needed to bring forth ideas that children have. Here are some to try:

1. Have you ever noticed that some people seem to remind you of animals? There is an older man on our street with tired, friendly lines in his face, sort of like a basset hound. I've always liked him.

2. "Boy, do I wish I had stayed at home," I said to myself. "Coming along on this excursion was a real mistake!" Little did I know how I was to feel about it later.

3. We were just sitting there on the beach, right at the place where the wet sand ended and the dry sand began. We had been sitting there for a long time, talking about nothing in particular, and only the highest waves came very near to us.

4. Ever since I could remember, I had been fascinated by the big grandfather clock. I used to sit for hours, watching the pendulum or the hands, or trying to see pictures in the grain of the wood.

5. Everyone says that all cats are graceful. I thought this was true, up until the time that Puddy came to live at our house.

6. Bill walked to the window to let in a little air. As he began to raise it, something caught his eye. He stood with his mouth open. There on the lawn below was the strangest thing he had ever seen.

7. At first the noise was very faint and seemed far away. It was an odd noise, one that the men didn't recognize. As it moved closer they went out to see what it might be.

8. The children were playing on the beach when they found the strange footprints in the sand. Their curiosity got the best of them and they decided to follow the tracks along the shore.

9. Mary knew that if her parents found out, she wouldn't be able to sit for days, but she was determined to carry out her plan in spite of this.

10. Closer and closer our ship came to this strange new world. I waited tensely, fearing unknown things, yet at the same time listing in my mind a hundred unanswerable questions. What would I see? What would I hear? What manner of creatures would occupy this place? What tastes and smells and textures would I learn to live with, of which I now knew nothing? And—most important of all—would our expedition be able to accomplish what we had set out to do?

11. The unfamiliar sound increased. Louder and louder it grew, seeming to surround us. We had stopped where we were when it started, and now stood looking at each others' faces. Each of us saw his own increasing fear reflected in the expressions of his companions. Louder still that unknown sound became, and louder again, beyond possibility. Suddenly, ...

12. "Once upon a time," I began my story. Then I paused to look at my little sister. I had Debbie's complete attention. She had already forgotten the broken television. "Long ago I knew a little girl," I said, "and do you know what? She looked almost exactly like you." I paused again. What kind of story would I make up? Debbie seemed to be certain I would tell a wonderful story. "Well, one time quite late at night . . . ."

13. Davey was shivering as he faced the steps of the deserted Thompson mansion. The sky was dark and gloomy and he knew it would be even darker and gloomier inside. If only Cliff had not dared him to go in by himself! He reached out and slowly opened the door.

14. Peering cautiously around a clover leaf, Eugene relaxed as he saw that the coast was clear. "Whew!" he thought. "That was a narrow escape for an elf!"

15. The last weak rays of the sun streaked coldly across the sky. Linda knew that soon the field would be swallowed by the rising fog and clammy darkness. She shivered and touched her heels gently to the horse's flanks. Then, without warning, they heard the scream above the sound of splintering and crashing.

16. As Little Running Fox neared the moss-covered swamp's edge, a huge bird with orange, purple, green, and yellow feathers darted into the bushes. Little Running Fox raced into the thick swamp, stumbling down a faintly trod animal path, searching for the bird.

17. Many frightening tales have been told about people who have taken the shortcut through the forest near our school. I usually walk around the tip of the forest to avoid taking the shortcut on my way home from school. But this particular day was special, because my grandmother was soon to arrive at my home. With scarcely a second thought, I decided to take the shortcut. I had not gone far when the coolness of the air and deathly silence surrounded me. Then I heard the cracking of a twig and the rustling of leaves behind me.

18. It was the bottom of the ninth inning. The score was tied, seven all. We had two men on base, two outs, and I was at bat. I had a decision to make now. I had been given the signal to bunt from the coach, because the infielders were playing

deep, and, although I don't normally brag, I am a good bunter. All season I had wanted to hit just one homer; if I could hit one now, we would win the final game of the season. On the other hand, if I did as the coach told me, we could load the bases and let the next batter try his skill. Either way there was the chance of my making the last out. Just as the pitcher released the ball, I made my decision.

19. "Well," said the little old lady, "I don't know how I will do it, but I must find some things to cook up in a stew for my family tonight." And so she tied her scarf around her head and went out into the yard.

All of the vegetables in her garden had already been harvested, but she decided to look where the rows had been. At the far end of the second row were two turnips which had not been found in the harvesting.

After she had started the boiling water and put the turnips in, the little old lady said, "I don't know how I will do it, but I must find some things to cook with these turnips in a stew for my family tonight." And so she again tied her scarf around her head and went out.

Finishing Story From a Beginning Paragraph

We were just sitting there on the beach, right at the place where the wet sand ended and the dry sand began. We had been sitting there for a long time, talking about nothing in particular, and only the highest waves would come very near us.

Then a high, high wave came in. It dropped off a treasure chest. We picked it up and tried the lock. We got a nail file, the lock opened easily. There was more than a million dollars. We jumped for joy, we yelled. Then my companion went over to the money, I was still yelling for joy. He discovered it was Confederate. Away went our black limousine. I found at the bottom of the chest a pirate's map. We studied it carefully. It was a map of Davy Jones' Locker. We went diving all day and all night. The gear cost us about $50, but we thought it would be worth it when we found the chest full of gold and jewels. We finally found it. We're millionaires, I gurgled. We pulled it ashore and opened the chest. In it was a note,

"Captain Kidder, ha ha!"

A fifth grade pupil

Starting by Writing Beginnings

Writing may also be started by having the class work as a group to invent the opening of a story. The story may then be finished by individuals or smaller groups within the class or exchanged with another class.

Writing story beginnings can be done on a purely mechanical basis, such as by listing unrelated phrases, selecting perhaps three to weave into a sentence, and then polishing the sentence (a good way to bring forth the merits of polishing!). For example, these unrelated phrases may be presented: a fleecy cloud, a bag of popcorn, a clap of thunder, a pile of dead leaves, the happily romping puppy, Easter vacation. If the class chooses the cloud, the thunder, and the puppy, they may first suggest a sentence such as, "Under a fleecy cloud, the happily romping puppy played until he heard the thunder." This may be polished and revised until it becomes much more sophisticated, as "All by himself, the puppy romped happily as the wind swept fleecy clouds across the sky overhead. Then, suddenly, came a sound he had never heard before—a clap of thunder." After discussion of the various ways in which the puppy might react and what he would then do, possibly listing words on the chalkboard, the class can be turned loose to write their various endings.

Random Phrases to Use

a dewy spider web
reversing his field
the spray from the speedboat
with siren screaming
the slurp of a suction pump
slamming the window
an enormous drumstick
pelting hail on the roof
sniffing at the door
swaying in the chilled air
the striking of the town clock

the car lurched
swerving into the other lane
rubbing the sunburn lotion
a tall man with red hair
a squeaking, rusty sound
the ragged coonskin cap
a smell like chocolate syrup
three gigantic steps
the old man's cave
a plain piece of white paper

The possibilities for points of departure for class-composed story beginnings are almost limitless—limited, if at all, only by the imaginations of the children.

As another approach, the class may wish to describe in detail the physical setting and then have individuals add their own characters and action. Settings might be suggested from the current interest in social studies or science; a tropical rain forest, the interior of a colonial frontier cabin, a fire station, a Hawaiian village, the bear cage at the zoo, a chemistry lab, a fox's lair, a California gold camp, the control tower at an airport, a weather station in Alaska, an Argentinian cattle ranch—almost anything can be utilized.

A different type of departure point may be established from the realm of literature appreciation. The mood or emotional climate may be described, after appropriate examples in the children's reading have been reviewed. The children may detail a feeling of physical elation, the kind of mood that comes with a surge of energy—the yen to run, to leap, to improvise vigorous choreography, perhaps even to shout. (According to many teachers this feeling is all too common among youngsters!) Or a mood of fear, of awesome impending doom, perhaps with a few appropriate bits of scenery (as in "The Fall of the House of Usher") can be built.

The serene beauty of a rural sunset, with its mood of tranquility, can be evoked. If the children feel this is too "corny," they may prefer to try describing the special feeling that comes with an "Open House" evening at school, the familiar corridors and entrances seen against the unfamiliar blackness of night, the shining of street and hallway lights, parents and little brothers seen anew against the backdrop of the classroom rather than at home.

Familiar Characters

Another sort of given beginning from which the children might work is using a character with whom they are already familiar. Such characterizations might be borrowed from nearly any source with which the children are familiar: a character from a story in one of the reading books, an historical figure, a well-known favorite from literature, a figure seen in the comics in the local newspaper, a personality frequently characterized on television, or even one of the lead personalities in, perhaps, a Walt Disney picture currently making the rounds of the local motion picture houses (if all the children have not actually seen the movie, they will probably have listened to discussions of it by those who have, and have watched the television advertisements for it). The writing might be about an imagined personal adventure with the character, about an imagined experience the character had with a friend, or just a story "made up" about the character.

Preparation for such a project may include a discussion of physical descriptions and the ways in which the character would react in different sorts of situations. Children will probably enjoy this type of activity most if they can project the character into their own environment. The following titles should give some indication of the possibilities:

The Day Tom Sawyer Painted My Fence
Peanuts and His Friends Attend a Dog Show in Our Town
Pinocchio in Our Playground
The Advice Ben Franklin Gave Us
Puss-in-Boots at the Supermarket
Thumbelina Helps the School Nurse
Flipper Helps a Friend of Ours
A Visit From George the Monkey

Paul Bunyan at City Park
Ali Baba and the Forty Surfers
The Seven Dwarves Shop for Christmas
The Secret Garden in the Suburbs
A Visit From Toad of Toad Hall
A Halloween Costume for Raggedy Ann
Jiminy Cricket, Substitute Teacher
Br'er Rabbit Gets a Traffic Ticket
How a New Friend Helps Johnny Tremain
Dr. Seuss Sent Me
Young Abe Lincoln Solves a Problem
The Further Adventures of Thomasina
The Beverly Hillbillies Go on a Vacation

In addition to stories about familiar characters, character sketches may be written. For these, depart from the worn-thin "My Favorite Teacher" and "My Younger Sister" and have them write about other characters perhaps equally familiar. For example:

The Attendant at Our Gas Station
Our Bus Driver
My Brother's Best Friend
Someone I'll Never Forget
A Magician I Saw Once
The Quarterback
Our Paper Boy

The central idea of character sketching is to bring to mind a picture of the character. This picture does not have to be complete in all details and it is well to keep this in mind, as the children are encouraged to write only a few sentences which give a basic picture, with the reader filling in more detail in his imagination as he reads. Another way to view this kind of character sketching is to call it "verbal snapshots" and to stress the idea of "at first glance."

The Fisherman

Down the old cobblestone street was a tumbled-down fish store owned by Mr. Tantillo. The store was old and peaceful looking, but inside it was more exciting. The clean counters were filled with fish of all kinds, all lined up in rows, smelling very nice, and in the corner the bread and other goods were kept.

To me, everything in the store seemed so exciting but the center of attraction was Mr. Tantillo.

His brown eyes seemed to have a kind, friendly and cheerful look. His huge nose seemed to stand out with his huge gray-black mustache underneath.

One thing about him was his smile. It gave him an even more friendly, jolly and loyal look. The wrinkles on his forehead gave him a look of honesty.

Even though he had little money, he was a happy, jolly, lovable, carefree man.

To me he was a very nice friend to have.

Everyone in town enjoyed him. They loved to hear him talk of his adventures. He talked with an Italian accent because he was born in Italy.

To the town he was everyone's friend, helpful, jolly, lovable, and nice—very, very nice.

Anna, grade 7

Using Objects

Showing specific objects to the class and eliciting responses to them is still another way for setting a class to writing, and first, of course, for getting ideas flowing. Not all responses to an object will be the same, nor should they be. True expression of individuality and creativeness will produce varied responses. For example, showing a beach hat may cause one pupil to write about his vacation and another to recall his working on the farm. This list of objects that may be shown is a beginning:

A pair of baby shoes
A bowling trophy

A shovel
A toy truck
A catcher's mitt
A well-chewed pencil
A bird cage
A well-worn wallet
A sextant
A silver dollar
An autograph book
An old family Bible
A welcome mat
A roller skate
A red bandana
A doll buggy
An alarm clock
A battered suitcase
Seeds
Shells
A box of buttons
A snail
A horseshoe
A bag of old shoes.

Following discussion about an object, one or more beginnings may be composed and written by the class or even an
entire group story written. With experience, children can write
stories independently merely from seeing and discussing an
object. Once again, lists of words related to the object and to
the writing topic are most useful for spelling help and for inspiration. Photographs or pictures may be used in much the same
manner as objects, and don't overlook the possibilities from
drawings made by children.

A repeated word of caution about using pictures (and
objects, pupil drawings, film, etc.) to stimulate expression: help
the children get ideas flowing by first asking for a few descriptive
words, by getting answers to a few questions, or by mentioning
a few things your imagination tells you.

More Suggestions

Many of the good ways to begin writing in a class defy classification. Some of these are presented here, in no particular order, as a smorgasbord for choosing at random or as springboards for other ideas.

1. Bring to class a newspaper story about a prominent personality familiar to most of the children. Use data from the news story as a reason for composing greeting cards which will actually be mailed (football player has his leg in a cast, cowboy star has a new horse, etc.).
2. After a field trip, record on the board the sounds the children said they heard. Rewrite the list with the children supplying more descriptive interpretations of these sounds. Follow with compositions about "The Sounds in (of, when, etc.)."
3. Retell a favorite story or legend. Have the children change the ending.
4. Have the children rewrite current events or news stories as a story written in the first person, i.e., as a personal experience.
5. Rewrite "And to think I saw it on Mulberry Street" in terms of a street in the community and a new set of made-up "sights."
6. Write a sequel to "Ping, the Duck."
7. Take a well-known story character, such as Cinderella, Daniel Boone, etc., and write a new adventure for him or her.
8. Read a story to the children, a few pages each day. After a number of episodes have been read, have the children write what they think the next episode will contain.
9. Use a silent film such as "People of the City," or run part of one without sound. Ask the children to write what they think happened to cause the action they saw.
10. Have children write a story to illustrate a proverb such as "All that glitters is not gold," or "Don't cry over spilt milk."
11. Make a display of paper dolls on a wall chart: use it as a group of people for a story. The children may name them,

give personalities, etc. This is best done as a project carried over from a number of lessons.

12. Have the children sit in a circle. One person can start off with a word, such as Oscar. The next child adds a word or phrase until a complete sentence is given. This can be continued until a complete story about the initial word is given.

13. After reading a few stories in an appropriate vein, have the children write one about why the zebra has stripes, why a porcupine has quills, etc.

14. Post pictures of various breeds of cats. Have the children write about their personalities and ways of doing things. Dogs, circus animals, baby pictures, etc., may be used.

15. Tell a story in a very colorless way. Ask the class to do a better job. This story could be used:

Joe wanted to surprise his family. He made hotcakes for breakfast with green food coloring in them. His family was startled, but they liked the hotcakes.

16. Show about half a dozen well-illustrated book jackets to the children. Have them write their own stories using the title and pictured material from one of them.

17. Cut an interesting news headline from the paper. Have a story to match it composed by a child or a group of children.

Picture Collection as the Basis for Story Writing

For this writing experience pictures of a tropical rainforest (*Life* magazine)[1] were used as the basis for motivating stories about the jungle. The pictures were discussed and left visible for study. The teacher drew a diagram on the board of a possible jungle layout, showing locations of a water hole, a clearing, a bamboo thicket, trails, and other features suggested by children. Animals which might be found in the jungle were suggested. Pupils found books in the library which illustrated them, and these were set up for display and study. "Describing words" were given and defined. Words in various categories were suggested by the teacher and solicited from the class and were

[1] Compiled in *The World We Live In*. New York: Time, Inc., 1955.

written down for reference. Example: "Snake: deadly, lethal, slithering, glittery-eyed, fangs, cobra, python," etc. Emphasis was on describing (descriptive) words, and children were encouraged to experiment, even stacking five or six adjectives in front of a noun.

The children then set to work writing "jungle stories." The results ranged greatly in quality and format. One girl wrote a lengthy, hackneyed account of a beautiful girl explorer and her exploits. Another child came up with a brief but original and beautiful piece covering five minutes in the life of a cobra snake. The children were given individual help by the teacher and by several "helpers" of good ability who finished early. Those with extra time made pictures or looked up more reference material in the class library. Evaluation of the story as a whole and of individual original phrases was made through discussion. Later experience showed that many words introduced in this lesson became a part of the children's reading and speaking vocabularies.

Building Blocks

Prose is architecture, not interior decoration.

Ernest Hemingway

The ideas in the previous chapter were meant as spring-boards for starting children to write and for eliciting further ideas from you. We hope that you will refer back to that chapter later for more of our ideas—and yours. But after you've once started, you need to know how to keep things moving, to keep writing projects fresh and interesting and challenging once your students have gotten a little experience.

Compare, for a moment, the process of learning to write with the way many first graders learn to read. At the start, they master a small group of words by sight. Then, after they have acquired some experience to which other learnings may be related, they begin on the basic principles which connect printed symbols with meaningful language. Similarly, in the writing progress of a teacher and class, there comes a time when they are ready to delve into some of the basic components of writing.

For purposes of organization in this matter, we shall make another comparison. We are going to liken the writer's trade to that of the carpenter. A carpenter needs to have a tool chest equipped with all the proper tools. He also needs materials with which to build. In a later chapter we shall inventory the contents of the writer's tool chest. In this one we shall discuss the building blocks of writing, those things which are to a writer as pine and redwood and nails and hardware are to the carpenter. These, then, are the materials, the building blocks, of language: words, sentences, the many forms writing can take, and the way to organize a story.

As you read the chapter, you will undoubtedly be thinking that we are supplying you with too much. We are not trying to tell you that the young writers in your classroom can become skilled craftsmen during one school year. Your children can't learn all of these things while they are in your charge, but if you are knowledgeable about the building blocks of language, you will be able to help them in specific ways when they need your help. If you doubt what we are saying, then keep firmly in mind the image of yourself teaching a woodworking class and standing by without helping as a youngster tries to construct a small jewelry chest out of rough two-by-fours.

Using Intrinsic Qualities of Words

Words have their own intrinsic qualities which can be used very effectively in writing. Some of these qualities of connotation are too elusive to be catalogued and the technique of using them belongs in the realm of "writer's instinct." Other qualities of words can be more definitely pinned down, and hence the techniques of using them can be taught. Some words have emotional coloring (or lack it) related to their derivation. Many of our words dealing with the most elemental facts of living come from old English: *home, wife, fight, woe.* Many other words seem "deemotionalized" and come to us from Latin, such as *ecclesiastic.*

A Word Chart (for Developing More Precise Vocabulary in Describing Objects—Children Add to the Lists)

Color	Pattern
pale	irregular
vivid	flowered
apple	parallel

Size	*Shape*
tiny	spherical
elephantine	conical
microscopic	round

Condition	*Sound*
weathered	cushioned
shining	soft
dull	harsh

Texture	*Taste*
silky	sour
rough	bitter
furrowed	buttery

Odor	*Motion*
musty	swirling
rancid	rhythmic
fresh	

The effect words can achieve comes also from their length. Short words are generally forceful and connote more action, particularly when used in short sentences. Longer words and more intricate sentences can convey a mood, or be used to space out sections of faster action. An interesting activity is to have children think up word bands, for example, setting down a spectrum from "dashed" to "traversed rapidly."

Polly Puckerup parted from her patio, paced past Patrick Way where she pivoted and proceeded pokily to Pat's Pizza Parlor where she sat till she got fat.

Gayle, grade 4

There are a number of interesting projects involving words for more gifted or ambitious children above the primary grades. These include collecting phrases from foreign languages, or working with terms from our own language which are not general but belong to perhaps the U.S. Navy, jazz musicians, cowboys, etc. Elizabethan English is rich in colorful compound words—addlepate, skinflint, etc. Coined phrases and commercial brand names also provide food for the thoughtful. An interesting idea for practice in either written or oral work is to attempt to use the language of a particular type of person—a Forty Niner, an old lady who is ill, a fighter pilot.

One of the skills in working with words is knowing the very best and most exact way of getting across an idea. Well-equipped writers don't have to grope for a word; they choose one. Some study of synonyms comes up with routine class work, but much more can be done. The children should be introduced to a thesaurus, and one or more obtained for classroom use if at all possible. (Some children may be able to purchase their own in the pocket edition.) Group contests in naming synonyms are an excellent "indoor sport," providing challenge for the best and enlarging small vocabularies for some of the rest. Another good activity is to study advertisements for color words, noting differences among car ads, clothing and cosmetic ads, etc.

Lessons in the use of adjectives, verbs, and adverbs have long been a standby, but more work here is also quite worthwhile. Lists of words suggested by the class to describe a certain type of climate, or the exact ways certain animals move about are excellent preparation for the preciseness needed in writing a story. Time spent by the group in a "What words will we need for a story about this?" session is always invaluable for providing inspiration and spelling help for those who need it. Or, the class can play some of the old familiar games, like "How did the boy go home?" (He ran, skipped, shuffled along, etc.)

Word Lists to Help Describe Setting:
Jungle Stories (Fourth Grade)

Climate	*Colors and Sights*	*Feelings*
tropical	darkish green	scarey
damp	shadowy	feeling of fear
humid	filtered sunlight	an evil place
warm	brown slimy mud	danger
moist	shadowy things	spooky
oppressive	canopy of trees	eerie

hot
sticky
dank
thirsty hot
too hot to wear a shirt
    and too sticky not to

twisting vines
cannot see very far
plant life everywhere
ooze
occasional ray of sun-
    shine

Sounds
bird calls
distant chattering of monkeys
slithering sounds
walking in muddy water
quiet sound of a snake moving
rustle of leaves
a slow-moving river is almost silent
buzzing of insects

Smells
dank
stinky
rotting leaves
blossoms of jungle trees (vines)
animal spoor
a green, growing smell

Animals
monkeys: chattering, energetic, swinging through trees
snakes: slithering, deadly, lethal, glittery-eyed, slow-moving (anaconda)
parrots: brightly colored, noisy, sharp curved beaks
insects: buzzing gnats or mosquitos, dangerous ants, leeches, horrify-
    ing, disgusting, shiny dragonflies

Sentences

As most teachers and many children know, there are any
number of things which can be done with the arrangement of a
sentence. The order of a sentence can be played with, as:

I went home slowly.
Slowly I went home.
Home I went, slowly.
Slowly home I went.

Or later, with variations such as these:

While Mother baked the birthday cake, my brother
wrapped the presents and I arranged the table.

I arranged the table as Mother baked the birthday
cake and my brother wrapped the presents.

Mother baked the birthday cake, I arranged the
table, and my brother wrapped the presents.

Sentence rearranging is best done as a class or group activity, and then followed by encouraging children to vary
sentence patterns in their written work. It should be pointed out
to children that in longer sentences, the most important idea or
information should be given stress by putting it either at the
beginning or the end of the sentence.

Another form of sentence practice for whole-class work is
"building."

I can run.

I can run fast.

I can run faster than you.

Let's have a race to see if I can run faster
than you.

Though these kinds of practice with sentences cover only a
small portion of the subject "What Can Be Done with Sentences,"
they are a good starting point. When children have had enough
experience with and enjoyment from playing around with sentences, they may be led to a more comprehensive and sophisticated survey of sentences per se.

For instance, sentences may be classified (and so often
tediously are) according to the intent of the speaker as declarative, interrogative, imperative, and exclamatory. And they are
often, in like manner, classified by grammatical construction as
simple, complex, or compound.

There is another system of classification generally less
familiar—and a little more subjective—but potentially much more
useful to young writers and their teachers. This is based on the
"shape" in which the thought is presented. Sentences may be
prosaically just a string of words in ordinary style:

I played in the park and Mother shopped.

I gave my sister her lunch and put her down for a nap.

The same sentences can be "shaped" a little to "tilt" toward the ending, thus giving it more importance:

While Mother shopped I went to play in the park.
It was after I gave sister her lunch that I put her
down for a nap.

More interestingly, ideas may be balanced in opposition:

Mother shopped, but I played.
Kittens are soft; their claws are not.
The sand was hot, the ocean cold.

Another trick with style is the repetitive sentence, with three or more things said in the same way:

March brings the wind, April has showers, and May
gives us soft sunshine.
Father walked briskly, I tried to match his strides, and
Jimmy followed along as fast as his legs could carry him.

It is possible, once a class group has experimented with sentences and played around with their various effects, to make a resource list of the different classifications of sentences and ways of varying their arrangement. This could then be used for reference during writing projects, particularly during the re-writing or "polishing" stages. If a class is only reasonably inter-ested in the "playing around with sentences" phase, however, the amount of time required to make such a list might be better spent in other activities and occasional review sessions.

Finally, sentences—like words—must be used in relation to their surroundings and with the mood and intent of the writer kept in mind. Long, leisurely sentences may be strung together. Short, staccato sentences are used to tell of swift action. Or a two- or three-word sentence may be placed at the end of a long expository one to give force to one idea.

There is one other aspect of the sentence-writing game which children generally enjoy (under proper circumstances)—

punctuation. Young writers should be encouraged to explore the possibilities not only of periods, commas, and question marks—having undoubtedly already discovered the joys of the exclamation point—but also of colons, semicolons, dashes, parentheses, and quotation marks. The proper circumstances for learning their use should include as little rule-recitation as possible. When the need arises, a model or models should be found to copy. This works particularly well with quotation marks.

Using Various Writing Forms

It is doubtful that any teacher would limit his or her class's opportunities for composition to "What I Did Last Summer." However, teachers rarely consider the full range of forms which writing can take when selecting writing projects. In this section we list a number of forms which any professional writer might consider using to express an idea or fill an assignment, with the hope that teachers reading this book will scan the list with an active rather than a passive mind. By this we mean considering each item in terms of various content—including social studies, science, art, and music—to be taught during the year, the instructional needs of the class, their areas of special interest, and also the various uses to which the finished projects might be put.

In addition to just "writing a story" children may express their creativity in some of the following forms:

Autobiography

This is an excellent way to get acquainted at the beginning of the year. Children may prefer to focus only on a portion of their lives or on only one area of activity—an experience during summer vacation as a Little Leaguer, school life, etc. Some structuring, such as limiting the scope of the topic, will probably be necessary. Otherwise, you may find that the children do little more than find out from their parents the name of the hospital in which they were born and the street addresses of the homes in which their family has lived and provide you with this list. If you do not choose to ask the children to limit the scope of their writing, you might instead ask them to include certain types of information and provide them with a list such as the following, from which they may choose an appropriate number of items to cover.

1. Did I tell whether or not I like my first name (or nickname)?
2. Have I included something about the people in my family that would let people know what they are like?
3. Did I tell about a pet, toy, or pastime that I have enjoyed very much?
4. Did I tell what I look like?
5. Can I tell some way in which I have changed in the last year or two, such as something I didn't used to like but do like now?
6. Do I want to tell what is the earliest thing I can remember?
7. Could I tell what I want to be when I grow up, and my reasons for wanting this?

My Life

I was born in Roseville. When I was two, I used to play with my toys. I often played with my big brother's toys, too. When I was three I had a little brother. I played with my little brother when I had nothing to do. When my big brother got home from school he played with me. When I was four I played with my toy truck. I liked to play with toys very much. My little brother often played with my toys. And I played with his toys also. When I was five I went to school for my first time. My big brother was in third grade. When I was six I was in first grade. My big brother was in fourth grade. When I was seven I was in second grade. I read a lot of books. I liked to read. My little brother was four. Now that I'm eight I'm in third grade. I played two square and tether ball. I like school.

Donnie, grade 3

Biography

This is obviously a good ploy for social studies enrichment. Children may enjoy telling in their own words the life of Benjamin Franklin, Franz Liszt, John Kennedy, or any one of a number of famous persons. They may wish to invent a person—a pioneer child traveling west in a covered wagon, or a defender of the Alamo—and tell of that person's life in terms of historically valid information. Biographies needn't be limited to human beings. Many children will delight in the opportunity to write in biographical form of a beaver who lived in the Columbia River a hundred years ago, of their pet dog, or perhaps George Washington's favorite horse. (Remember the popularity of the book *Ben and Me*.)

Diaries or Journals

These can be realistic, with children individually, in groups, or as a class making entries in the "diary" of any historic or contemporary figure. Before beginning, the children should be well equipped with enough information to make their writing vivid and interesting. Christopher Columbus, Teddy Roosevelt, a Peace Corps worker—the entire population of our world, past and present, can provide subjects. The kinds of background information which can be provided are likewise varied. If, for example, Sir Francis Drake is to be the subject, providing background information can go far beyond reading a sketch of his life from the encyclopedia. Research should be presented (by the teacher and/or the children) covering the details of his era necessary to make the diaries come alive. This might include information on Elizabethan dress, manners, seamanship, and so forth, plus information on the specific area of exploration or episode of his life to be covered. Excerpts from the journal kept by Drake's chaplain Francis Fletcher might be read to the class. (This can be obtained in most large libraries.) Realism is not the only note which can be sounded in diaries, however. Less obvious and more whimsical might be a diary of Santa Claus, Humpty Dumpty, a spare tire, the family pet, Satan, a cartoon character, a leprechaun, or an octopus. Preparation will still be needed, in the form of class discussion: What does the character like? Where and how does he live? What other characters might be included? Also, what useful words should be listed for all the children to see? Finally, have some of the children discuss a few of the elements they think they will include in their stories and how they will begin, in order to further stimulate the imagination of all of the children.

Letters and Greeting Cards

Nearly every class at one time or another has written to a classmate kept at home by illness or one who has recently moved away. Most children, too, get at least one exposure to the process of writing away for materials or information. What else can be done with letter writing? What about greeting cards? Greeting cards made by children can be thought of as just another form of the social letter; in fact, it is one which can be less demanding of language arts skills and more demanding in terms of creativity. Letters or greeting cards may be sent to the custodian if he has sprained his wrist, to a favorite baseball player if he has just had a winning (or losing) streak, to other children in the school, after Christmas vacation to friends or relatives who have sent gifts (mothers will bless you); letters to editors may be written on current issues large or small, and so on.

Do not overlook the fact that a series of letters is an excellent way to tell a story—one that is repeatedly used by professional writers. This is one form of fiction writing or report making which lends itself well to group endeavor.

Scripts

Whether the subject is fiction or nonfiction, children usually enjoy organizing materials in script form. This can be either for a play, radio, television, or motion picture. Models for copying format are most helpful. Children must think their material through and edit out irrelevant detail, whether they are preparing a script for a weather report, fire prevention commercial, children's story hour, you-are-there documentary, or ghost story. Again, this lends itself well to group endeavor.

Material Which Is Serialized or Written in Installments

Regardless of content, this can be fun. Many classes enjoy writing weekly installments to a cliff-hanging adventure series (allowing time between installments to mull over possible solutions to predicaments and new predicaments for the next one). Information about school activities can be reported to parents in installments, each covering a different topic—an excellent Public Schools Week activity. Writing a column about school or class affairs is another installment activity which can prove profitable—outlets can perhaps be found in the school newspaper, the PTA bulletin, local shoppers news, or a bulletin board in the hall.

A wide variety of kinds of writing can be serialized, but "in installments" is not all by itself a writing style. Before beginning, it might be wise to provide examples of the kind of material being covered. With any form of fiction narrative, the many children's programs on television which are serialized can be cited. Also the techniques discussed later in this chapter in "Organization of a Story" might well be checked over.

Why the Birds Fly South

Once upon a time there was an old bearded bird who heard from a young chipper bird that there was lots and lots of bird seed in the south.

Of course he was kidding about it, but the old bearded bird believed him. So he flew away. He flew and flew but he was old and had to stop once in a while. Once he stopped on an island. He decided that he would stay there for a while. He thought about all the bird seed he would be eating. So he flew across the wide blue sea. Finally he got to the south. But he did not find lots and lots of bird seed, he found something better.

He found heat! All of a sudden he remembered all the hard winters he had. He told all the birds about the heat so everybody went to the south and thats why the birds fly south.

Tim, grade 4

Forms of Poetry

Examples of various forms of poetry in which children have found success are included with this chapter. We do not mean to imply, however, that these are the only ones which can easily be used, or that forms are the most important aspect. The form of a poem is only an aid to expressing content. For most poetry writing, children need to be directed away from a preoccupation with making words rhyme towards a concern for the expression of emotion or vivid imagery. *It is the idea which is important.*

Despite the fact that expression of emotion and writing of poetry are often highly individual, even private, endeavors, much can be done to help children get started. For example, bring something—anything—to class, even a weed picked on your way to school. Ask the class to list as many words or phrases as they can to tell how ugly or beautiful it is. Then review the list, asking the children to help you mark the contributions which are unique and appropriate. Then opinion may be gathered as to what emotion can be symbolized by the weed and what moods might be stimulated by studying it. List these also, soliciting opinion as to the most interesting. The class is then ready, either individually or as a group, to put ideas into poetic form—cinquain, haiku, or whatever they choose or wish to devise. Some children may enjoy trying out one poetic idea in a variety of forms.

Writing Cinquain—A Kind of Dwarf Poem

First line: one word, giving title.
Second line: two words, describing title.
Third line: three words, expressing an action.
Fourth line: four words, expressing a feeling.
Fifth line: one word, a synonym for the title.

Ballerina

Graceful lady
Whirling and gliding
Pavlova on stage now
Dancer.

Geraldine, age 9

Dove

White, soaring
Wings flapping, whirring
My heart lifts up
Bird.

Debbie, age 9

Deer

Sleek, graceful
Running and leaping
Happy to be free
Buck.

Susan, age 8

Bacon

Crisp, delicious
Frying and spattering
Waiting to be eaten
Breakfast.

Donald, age 8

Writing Limericks. Lines 1, 2, and 5 are rhymed, and lines 3 and 4. The rhythm is best taught by example. (The *Rotarian* magazine each month has a limerick section and contest.)

A puppy whose hair was so flowing
There really was no means of knowing
Which end was his head,
Once stopped me and said,
"Please, sir, am I coming or going?"

A cheerful old bear at the zoo
Could always find something to do.
When it bored him to go
On a walk to and fro,
He reversed it, and walked fro and to.

Said the condor, in tones of despair:
"Not even the atmosphere's rare.
Since man took to flying,
It's really *too* trying,
The people one meets in the air."

Oliver Herford

Writing Haiku. Haiku is a Japanese verse form consisting of three lines totaling seventeen syllables. It is usually on some subject in nature and has only the necessary words. The first and last lines have five syllables and the second line has seven.

> The bright dragon-fly
> Moves swiftly over water
> Racing his image.
>
> 7th grade

Writing Other Verse Forms. Couplet: Try giving the first line and having the pupils add a second line. Be sure to use an easy rhyming last word.

> Leaves are falling to the ground
> With a gentle, rustling sound.

Triplet: Begin with a list of rhyming words, for example: play, gay, may, say, hay, day.

> Our pup likes to play.
> He's clumsy, but gay.
> "Chase me" his eyes say.

Sijo is a Korean form similar to Haiku. It may express any emotion, is often related to nature, and may make use of opposites, humor, or realism. It sometimes has three lines, with 14 to 16 syllables per line, and is sometimes written as six short lines.

Fairy Tales, Fables, Myths

After studying examples of one or another of these forms, children will be quick to note the types of events and characters which typically appear in fairy tales, the kinds of sayings on which fables are based, or the sorts of events which myths seek to explain. For a first attempt, they may wish to precede the writing with the agreement that their fairy tale may concern a castle atop a mountain, two hard-working brothers, a wicked ruler, and a magical belt—or with a discussion of the possible ways in which one axiom can be illustrated, or with the agreement that they will invent a myth to explain why a horse has a name.

Tall Tales

After children have heard about John Henry or Paul Bunyan they can hardly be stopped from writing tall tales. Try encouraging having the main character be something besides an oversized strong man. Just as tall a tale could be told about one who was so wide he spread doors as he went through them, or one who becomes invisible (à la "My Favorite Martian").

Review Writing

Although this is generally thought of as an adult preoccupation, we should stop to consider how often children regale others with accounts of television programs or motion pictures, and yet how difficult it seems to arouse any real interest in them in giving book reports. Why not introduce children to reviewing via reports on television programs and local theatrical productions in the local newspapers, as well as book reviews from Sunday supplements and magazines? Once standards have been set by class projects, written or sometimes oral reviews (using notes) may be presented on recent television programs, offerings at the local theaters, school plays, books in the school library, or smaller programs presented within the school.

Advertising

Children are confronted with advertising at every turn and generally enjoy making up their own advertisements. You needn't confine yourself to bulletin boards on fire prevention or posters on healthful foods. Children can practice their skills with alliteration or internal rhyme to think up silly slogans for fictitious products. They can investigate the facts behind the near-deception in advertising for "nutritious" candy bars or the aspirin firm which boasts "You can't buy better than . . ." They can study the art principles which underlie an eye-catching poster or billboard and create their own—with an appropriate concise slogan—for a school play, safety campaign, etc. They can study the various types of color words used in advertisements for ladies' clothing, paint colors, and so forth, and perhaps try their hands at copywriting.

Icannagoo Pork and Beans

This luscious combination of fat, plump beans and juicy, tender chunks of pork is a mouth-watering treat for everyone in your family. Mr. Icannagoo sharply demands perfect quality in his excellent products. He will accept only the best of seasonings, such as pungent, imported mustard; thick, red catsup; black, freshly-ground Indian pepper. You get all of this nutritious and filling favorite food for the modest price of 39¢ for one sixteen-ounce can. The crowded lines are long at all busy counters, so hurry and find your place in a line. You will see that your trip to the store was very worthwhile when you get home to your kitchen and smell Icannagoo Pork and Beans bubbling on the stove. Get some soon before it is too late!

Bob, grade 6

Jokes and Riddles

These can frequently give exercise to children's imagination and creativity and can be fitted nicely into odds and ends of classroom time. How to get started? The children will often provide a start themselves with whatever is the latest joke craze. If not, jokes and riddles can be found aplenty in children's magazines and similar sources. Children often enjoy trying to create a joke or riddle by making variations on an example.

Parodies

Children love to make their own versions of familiar verse and songs. For example, many are only too familiar with the version of "Battle Hymn of the Republic" which begins "Mine eyes have seen the glory of the burning of the school . . ."

Many children, too, are Allan Sherman fans. Perhaps with good reason, many teachers would just as soon steer clear of adaptations in this vein. But most classes will enjoy taking a familiar melody and composing new words for a school or class song. Almost any occasion can become the reason for writing words to a song. Why not compose a Halloween song to "In the Hall of the Mountain King," or, if the well-liked cafeteria manager is leaving, a song of praise set to "The Girl That I Marry," or at the end of the school year, take a well-known folk song, create one verse about each child in the room, or one verse about each noteworthy event during the year.

News Stories or Feature Articles

Regardless of whether the class or school is "publishing" a newspaper, children will often enjoy writing news stories concerning events of interest. Teachers should remember the distinction between a "straight" news story and a feature article. A regular news story deals with facts in a straightforward manner, summarizing concisely at the beginning and then relating details. A feature article often involves a "human interest" angle, may interject more of the writer's personal attitudes or experiences with the situation, and may start with a "narrative hook" instead of the regular news story's concise statement of the most salient facts. For example, a news story about flood damage in a river community would begin with a summary of the damage done and give information about rainfall, flood stages of the river, and official action to alleviate suffering and remedy damage. A feature article might start with a description of a little boy in a rowboat, clutching his soggy teddy bear, and continue by relating the experiences of one particular family during the flood.

In order to acquaint children with journalistic style, a number of examples taken from newspapers for study and kept for reference as needed will probably be of much more value than ten lengthy, teacher-provided explanations. Children at the primary level will probably be able to tackle the simplest group projects on subjects in which they are quite interested, but older children, once they have become acquainted with the format, may wish to use it in a variety of ways. Fourth graders, for example, may wish to write news stories about an historic event they have studied, such as California's Gold Rush. Sixth graders, if they are working on a science unit on weather, may wish to prepare weather reports or news stories about unusual weather.

With any of these forms of writing, the problems of explaining to the children the exact nature of a specific form of writing can best be solved by presenting a number of examples from literature, current periodicals, or whatever is appropriate. In many cases children may be interested in searching out their own examples as further illustrations. It is also useful to save copies of children's work in a particular form to be used as an example and yardstick for subsequent classes.

Organization of a Story

This section covers the outlining and preplanning of a story as is usually done by professional fiction writers, and includes plotting, characterization, mood (atmosphere) and setting, tense, and point of view. Elementary teachers may have already decided that this material would be more suitable for some other level, but more can be done with elementary children in this area than is generally supposed.

Group Story: Seventh and Eighth Grade Reading Group

Why the Rattlesnake Has Rattles

"Now, remember," said the Old Woman Rattlesnake to her littlest Child Snake, "don't bite yourself."

"I'm not going to," said Child Snake, as she pushed him along with her snout, "and you don't have to push me, either."

So he scooted out of the old log they lived in and started off down the road.

"Just you remember," she called out after him. "Don't bite yourself. I don't want to stay up half the night taking care of you again."

Child Snake didn't answer her, but just scooted down the road a little faster. When he got bored, he took hold of his pointy tail in his mouth, being careful not to bite, and made himself into a hoop. Then he went rolling and hoopy-rolled himself halfway down the hill.

He stopped when he got to the old hole where all the gopher snakes lived, and laid himself out flat and still. They were, he saw, all slithering around down there, not doing anything that took any particular brains. Child Snake just stayed there a while kind of looking them over.

Well he had nobody else to play with, so he hitched himself on down, and crawled in with the pile so they would think he was any old gopher snake.

"Hey, whyn't we play tag?" Child Snake said to all those gopher snakes, and he dove into the pile going up and down and in and out like he was going to weave himself a mat. All those gophers were looking around and trying to keep track of their tails and hollering, "Who's It?"

Child Snake had a happy smile on his face, even if he couldn't smile very wide because he wasn't planning on letting his fangs show.

"I am!" he said, still weaving in and out, and he looked around for a likely tail to bite. It was a lot of fun being mean to these empty-head cousins, and he wasn't about to spoil his fun thinking about how maybe he shouldn't be doing this.

And there, right in front of him, was the likeliest-looking tail he thought he'd ever seen. So he leaned down, letting his fangs show at last, and he gave that tail a real chomping on.

All of the gophers (they saw right off what kind of snake he really was) lit out in all directions. And that left Child Snake right down in that hole chewing on his very own tail.

You can believe that he went off for home a whole lot quicker than he came, and Old Woman Rattlesnake had to stay up with him most all of the night.

"Just setting your mind to remember don't do you much good," she scolded at Child Snake next morning. "We got to fix your tail so's you'll know it don't belong to any gopher snake."

So she took and sewed a bunch of rattly old buttons right on the end of his tail.

This worked so well that ever since, to keep away from having to stay up all night with children who can't recognize their own other ends, the rattlesnake mothers took to having their children born with buttons on the ends of their tails.

The class as a group can enjoy and gain a great deal from preplanning a story. As a matter of fact, most teachers would be very hard pressed to find class time to take the group beyond the planning stages of a story. (*Quo Vadis* wasn't built in a day either.) Some children may be capable of working on their own individual stories after a group story-planning session. Plenty of working time should be allowed over a period of days and even weeks, and, in addition, the teacher should allow enough time for helping, followed by time for the class to appreciate the finished writing.

One of the easiest ways to start a story is to decide who the people in it will be and then to make a complete description of each major character. First, list the character's vital statistics, then begin on personality traits and typical ways they are expressed. If, for example, a girl is characterized as nervous, how does she act? Is she a Kleenex shredder? Does she constantly wiggle her feet, slipping her heel in and out of her shoe? Characteristic speech mannerisms should also be set down, and also each major character's attitude toward other major persons in the story. Much of this sort of material may be set down in finished sentences, or even paragraphs, with the idea that it is all ready to use wherever it seems to fall naturally into place in the story.

Plotting should not be made unnecessarily complicated for children. Most classes would probably do better simply making a list (perhaps tentative) of the sequence of events. Although the children are not introduced to the concepts of struggle, climax, or denouement, they should be asked to end the story quickly after the most important part of the action is done.

Mood and setting can generally be preplanned also. Children are most interested in the physical setting. This can be planned in detail, whether or not the group plans to actually complete a story. A map of the locale and diagrams of houses and places of business are devices employed by professional writers when preparing a story. If a past or future time period is involved, details of clothing, means of transportation and communication, etc., should be carefully checked, or invented if the story is to be set in the future.

When children have finished this they may be ready to establish the mood or atmosphere of the story and its pace—whether swift-moving adventure, perhaps, or more quiet, and possibly sad or romantic.

Uniformity of style can also be planned. Is the story to be told as if it has already happened (past tense) or as if it is happening right now? These are sometimes combined by the use of flashbacks. In planning uniformity of style the group should also consider who tells the story, or in whose thoughts and reactions the action takes place. This is called point of view. The story may be told in the first person by one of the characters, or told in the third person, but still telling it through the point of view of one of the characters. These are usually the two easiest ways. However, stories can be told from an omnipotent point of view, shifting from person to person and relating the inner thoughts of each.

With this much preparatory work, a story can "get written" by a fairly capable child without too much difficulty. If the series of lessons ends here, the children have still gained considerably in their knowledge and a few may try later tackling a story on their own. There are some other factors to be considered in organizing a story, but perhaps they are best saved until after the story has been completed and then considered along with the more routine checking for spelling, punctuation, and so forth.

Here is the checklist you might use:

1. Were unnecessary details kept out?
2. Were all necessary details included, or was a large part of the story left "inside the author's head"?
3. Did the beginning of the story have a "narrative hook" to pull the reader into the story? Should one be added, via flashback or some other means? Did the beginning of the story give some idea of who the hero is, what he is doing, when and where he is doing it?
4. Is the story in proportion? Every incident, conversation, and description must play its role and should have emphasis in proportion to its importance.
5. Have events happened too fast? Do they fall on each other in

a jumble, with no opportunity for the reader to anticipate or be reminded that an event has happened?

6. Is the dialogue brief and natural?

7. Is the story style consistent—breezy, formal, etc.—throughout?

Tools of the Writer's Trade

It's knowing what to do with things that counts.

Robert Frost

An integral part of creativity is the urge to experiment with the materials and tools at hand. In the previous chapter we discussed the building materials of language. Now it is time to explore the writer's tool chest. A carpenter, even though he may have the finest variety of lumber at his disposal, will not be able to build much of anything unless he knows how to use with skill his hammer and saw, brace and bit, and other tools. And an artist, even though well endowed with innate talent, may achieve little unless he is familiar with the uses of his pencils, charcoal, water colors, and oils. It is the same with writing. Thus, to help beginning writers, we must acquaint them with a variety of ways in which to use words and then give them ample opportunity to practice the techniques and skills we have shown them.

Some writing tools of importance to professional writers—personification, onomatopoeia, alliteration, internal rhyme, and the various forms of metaphor and analogy—are discussed in this chapter. These are the skills and techniques of the writer-creator, and they may be used even by the beginner. It may well be that these are the most important things we can teach the writing child and that childhood is the best time for learning them. Many teachers of creative writing who work with adults feel that, although most of their students can eventually learn to create a believable character and move him through a plausible story, the ability to use effectively all kinds of metaphor and figures of speech is a rare gift and belongs only to the finest of writers.

As much as readers of this book should expect children to be creative in their use of writing tools, they should also expect themselves to be creative in interpreting the contents of this chapter. Although examples of children's work will be given to illustrate our points, it is the purpose here to explain general principles rather than to give specific recipes. A number of very exact ideas for writing projects are given elsewhere in this book, but they should serve mainly as further explanations of some of the suggestions we make and as aids to teachers in getting themselves and their classes started. Too, the tools described in this chapter should be used in combination with the unique needs and talents of each teacher and class.

It should be noted that before, during, and after the children have been acquainted with these various tools which writers employ, such tools and techniques can be very profitably discussed in literature appreciation lessons. Teachers in the primary grades should not feel that this is a matter for teachers of older children only: many of these techniques are quite simple in nature and can readily be found in the best-loved literature for young children. Seeing how they have been employed by other writers in a variety of situations is one of the best ways to learn how these tools might be used. In addition, it might be profitable to keep in the classroom a checklist of the tools of the writer's trade which have been explored, as a reference when children are working on writing projects or to point to when examples are discovered in the literature children enjoy.

When classes first begin to experiment with these writing techniques, they will most likely overuse them. One child preoccupied with the use of adjectives wrote: "It was a roasting, muddy, sweaty day. There was a bony-headed, glittery-eyed snake in the jungle. One day this blue, squeezing, powerful, slick, slithering, crawling, scooting, dangerous, sliding, poison-spitting snake stared at me." When attention is called to any one technique, such Frankensteins may result. So much the better. In a short while the children's own sense of proportion should overcome such overuse, and the writing technique will then become a part of the child's array of writing skills, ready for use when needed.

Children May Make Lists of Words to Use

Words to Use Instead of Said

sobbed	claimed		
declared	informed		
suggested	smiled		
argued	blurted		
cried	mumbled		
questioned	observed		
bragged	warned		
corrected	snapped		
inquired	advised		
asked	glared		
began	told		
called	reminded		
ordered	stated		
wept	retorted		
sighed	gulped		

Noise Words

thump	squeal
purr	giggle
murmur	scrunch
crash	giggle
boom	tinkle
bang	chuckle
thud	bump
pop	thunder
splash	squeak
crack	patter
sigh	slurp

Words About Weather

cold	blustery
foggy	cloudy
windy	sunny
clear	rainy
cool	stormy
hurricane	hot
humid	warm
dry	sultry
changeable	snowy
tepid	stifling
misty	

What Airplanes Do

crash	streak
vibrate	roar
buzz	rumble
zoom	climb
fly	land
float	dive
swoop	
flash	

Some of the seemingly simpler writing devices—personification, onomatopoeia, alliteration, and internal rhyme—are frequently employed in the cartoons so many children see on television. Regardless of their fancy names, these techniques are appreciated and learned easily by even the youngest children.

Personification

Personification is the granting of human characteristics to a nonhuman object. On terms familiar to small children, it is Mickey Mouse, Huckleberry Hound, or perhaps the North Wind pursing his lips to blow. Examples of personification also abound in the classic children's literature—the Gingerbread Man, Br'er Rabbit, the Cheshire Cat.

In a fifth grade class, after the teacher had explained the principle of personification and various children had suggested objects which they might like to personify, one boy wrote this story:

I am a car. My name is Stanley. My driver is mean to me. He drives me until I smoke. My feet get hot. He floods me when I can't start.

So, one day when he was taking a nap, I rolled myself down to a fire hydrant and parked. In about ten minutes a cop came and stuck a fifty-dollar ticket in the window.

He could not afford the money so he sold me to a nice driver.

In primary grades, the discussion time needs to be longer, and individual efforts, if they are attempted, need to be preceded by group work. The children's work will usually turn out to be highly imaginative.

One second grade teacher, after reading to her class a story involving personification, asked the children to list a number of objects which might be personified. To each object, one describing word was attached to tell what this object did that people do, or what kind of personality it might have. The class then voted to select half a dozen which they liked the best.

For the next lesson, the teacher had prepared a roll of paper to be used in a scroll theater, explaining to the children that they had a certain number of "frames" in which to complete a story, using these characters. For each frame, the teacher would call upon volunteers to suggest a sentence. These sentences (for each frame) were listed on the chalkboard, and the children voted for those which they liked the best. As the story progressed, the teacher found that she had to make very few suggestions about keeping the personifications "in character," but the children did need help in ending the story with all of the details successfully incorporated. The teacher helped by suggesting sentences which would take care of the situation and by asking the children to provide sentences which would perform the same service. Although several times the children voted to include the sentences provided by the teacher in the latter portions of the story, the story is by no means teacher-written or inspired: examination of it will show that these are indeed the original ideas of children.

This is the story of the talking horse, the talking house, the dancing red flowers, the walking starfish, the talking rabbit, and the angry rain cloud.

It was summer and everyone was swimming. The angry cloud felt mean and rained. The dancing red flowers began to grow because of the rain. The rain cloud went swimming to refill himself with water.

The angry raincloud has made the pool empty. He rains and fills it. The angry raincloud went back into the sky to wait for the starfish. He wanted to put him on his Christmas tree. The horse and the rabbit rescue the starfish. They take him into the house.

Why don't you put the dancing red flowers in a flower show? said the house. They are ten feet and twelve inches high.

The flowers won $420.01. They planted themselves by the house to say thank you. The horse, the rabbit and the starfish went off to spend the money for a Christmas party. They happen to catch the cloud and tie him up in the front yard.

At the party the starfish walks up the Christmas tree to be the star. And they all live happily.

After the story was completed, the teacher lettered the sentences in the frames and subsequently allowed the children

to illustrate the frames in their free time. This allowed many of
the children who had not been particularly active in contribut-
ing to the text to put the stamp of their own individuality on
the finished story. Then the class invited another second grade
to appreciate their handiwork, and later showed the story to
their parents. The story was kept in the room and shown by
individual children to classroom visitors and other children, thus
motivating some of the most reluctant readers to a reasonable
competency with the text of the story.

Onomatopoeia

Another tool of the writer's trade which gives children no
end of delight is onomotopoeia. This is the use of words which
sound like what they describe, such as *buzz, tinkle, whoosh,* and
so on. There are a variety of ways in which children of all age
groups can work with "sound-effect" words and incorporate them
into writing projects, while also adding to their enjoyment of
literature.

An interesting beginning with younger children is to list
the animal sounds conventionally found in children's stories and
the ways in which those sounds are spelled. It is a challenge
to children of any age to try to put down in writing the sound
effects they hear on television. Incidental benefits in terms of
the children's interest in spelling cannot be ignored. One fourth
grade teacher was most gratified to overhear two boys—both
laggard spellers—arguing during recess about the proper spelling of the sound produced by a Model T automobile horn. Both
were reasonably correct phonetically, one holding out for
ee-oo-ga and the other for *eeu-gah!*

Sound effects written down by others can be studied from
almost any source, from comic books to Edgar Allan Poe's "The
Bells." With a minimum of preparation by discussion and ob-
servation of examples, children can be encouraged to make their
writing projects more vivid with sound-describing words. For
example, one teacher who had been working with primary children in a summer school language arts class asked her group
to watch a television program about the Keystone Cops, part
of a series about the "golden age" of silent movies. Discussion

brought out the fact that much of the funniness of these old movies depended upon the quick pace at which silly things happened and the sound effects which accompanied the television presentation. The children wrote a group story in the Keystone Cops manner, which began:

Crash! Boom! Bang!
Two prisoners are escaping.
Clatter, tinkle, pop!
They have broken out of jail and the police start to chase them.
Bang! Bang! Bang! Bang-oing! go their guns.

Although this story idea was supplied by the teacher, it seemed to fit quite well with the interests of the children. Variant sound effects appeared quite often, such as the gun which went "bang-oing." This was an attempt on the children's part to spell out the ricochet echo so often heard on television westerns. As holds true when other writing techniques are first taught to children, the use of spelled-out sound effects tends to be exaggerated at first, but later slips into a more proportionate role in the children's writing production.

An example of onomotopoeia (grade five):

The Clangy Bangy Car

I

Once upon a time there was a clangy bangy car.
It went:
"Honk, honk!"
"Smash, bam!"
"Boom! Crackle!"
"E-e-e-e-e-e-e-e-e-e-e" (sound of brakes)

II

And the tire went POP!!!
Ca-poomp-ca-poomp went the car.
Right on a bridge.
And the air in the tire went
"P-s-s-s-s-s-s-s-s-s-s-s-s-s-s-s!"

Alliteration

Another professional writers' tool which is frequently used to spark up their work and which is easily recognized by children is the use of the same beginning sounds in a series of words. This is alliteration, a device which is not commonly taught until children are much older and are enrolled in a poetry, or perhaps a literature, appreciation class. It seems ridiculous to wait so long when children are so early exposed to Daffy Duck, Bugs Bunny, Simple Simon, and many others, especially when we stop to consider the number of reading lessons in the primary grades devoted to learning the various initial consonants and consonant blends.

One reading group working with initial consonant blends listed a great number of words which began with *fl*, and then experimented with working them into silly sentences. One which they all agreed was "best and most fun" was:

A butterfly can fly, flap, flutter, flop, flitter, flick, float, flip-flop and "floop" in a loop.

This teacher saved the silly sentences, which had been written lengthwise on strips of cash register tape, and posted them on the bulletin board as reading challenges. Later, when this group had more experience working with initial consonant blends, they combined their knowledge of alliteration with the use of adjectives and composed the following story:

Once upon a time there was a slithery snake on a muddy hill. He was on the top. He went slithering and sliding in the slooshy, sloshy, sticky, gooey mud. He slithered and slooshed and slid all the way to the bottom!

Admittedly, this group had more than usual experience with writing, but the only immediate guidance provided by the teacher was two lists of *sl* words saved from a previous lesson (one describing how snakes move and one describing the consistency of mud) and the suggestion that if the snake were to move through the mud, it would need beginning and ending locations.

For children too mature to work from Simple Simon or Bugs Bunny, any number of examples can be drawn from literature. Rudyard Kipling used alliteration with much effect in his *Just So Stories*. In the story of how the elephant got his trunk, the Elephant Child goes to the "great, gray, green, greasy" Limpopo River.

In a lighter vein, for "quickie" lessons—and at no detriment to their mastery of phonics or spelling—older children may enjoy giving themselves nicknames such as Jivey Jumping Jean, or Bilious Bill. Social studies texts can be peopled with such personages as Phoebe from Phoenicia, Humorous Humphrey from Himalaya, etc.

Internal Rhyme

Old Man Whiskery-Whee-Kum-Wheeze
Lives 'way up in the leaves o' trees.
James Whitcomb Riley

Another technique which children hear often when young, but so often must wait to learn about—if ever—until they are in high school, is internal rhyme. This is the use in the same line of two or more words which rhyme. Small children can readily appreciate that this is the device which gives many television cartoon characters catchy names, such as "Augie Doggie."

Children at all grade levels enjoy composing "the fat cat sat"-style of nonsense lines just for the silly, ear-catching effects. A good warm-up activity is the making of word chains, i.e., lists of rhyming words. For example, thinking of words to rhyme with *red*, or *trip*, or *sleet*.

Some first and second graders composed the following:

Rooty-tooty, I'm a beauty!

A fake snake gave me a slight fright.

I broke a wall with a ball and watched it fall.

I put a ring on and it started to sing along.

As with alliteration, it is helpful to keep word lists or short rhymes (strips of cash register tape are good for this). They may be posted on the bulletin board, perhaps with accompanying pictures for the nonsense rhymes. Later they may go home as trophies, once the children have mastered the reading of all the words.

Older children can be challenged with more esoteric starters for rhyming, such as *urbane, ignite,* or *pure*. Or perhaps they may wish to construct mnemonic devices, either using internal rhyme or alliteration or both. At this point it would seem logical to introduce examples from works such as those by Edward Lear or Ogden Nash. Also, many children will enjoy using a rhyming dictionary.

Related Ideas

Skill in the use of ideas in juxtaposition or in relation to each other is a necessary part of any professional writer's technique. Children should not be considered too immature to use these tools. As a matter of fact, in five minutes' time a second grader can progress much more quickly in the use of a simile than in the use of a carpenter's hammer. Besides similes, children can express ideas in relationships by using metaphors, comparison, and analogy. Some ideas for the use of hyperbole will also be explained in this section.

Simile, metaphor, and comparison differ in only minor ways. A simile expresses likeness by the use of such terms as *like, as,* or *so*. The snow on the mountains was like the white frosting on a cake. He ran as fast as the wind. Many similes can be turned into metaphors. If we say the snow was white frosting on the mountains we have used a metaphor. A comparison is just what its name says. For example, the hills of California remind me of the hills of Portugal.

When children begin working with comparisons, experience has shown that they will be more interested in the expression of ideas than in the fine distinctions, which is perhaps just as well. It seems pointless to try to run counter to such a current, if not downright pedantic. For example, no teacher in her right

mind should reject a beautiful figure of speech simply because it was not a simile containing *as* or *like,* as had been assigned.

An excellent way to start children working with compara-tive ideas is to compile with the class a list of all the old stand-bys. Surprisingly enough, quite a few of them will be un familiar to children. Such lists usually include the following:

pale as a ghost
red as a tomato (beet)
old as the hills
green as grass
quiet as a mouse
snug as a bug in a rug
bright as a new-minted penny
busy as a bee (beaver)
nutty as a fruitcake
hungry as a bear
dry as a bone
low as a snake's belly
poor as a churchmouse
black as ink (the ace of spades)

From this point, the children may go on to making up own expressions. Some fourth graders turned out the foll

> pale as a dead flower
>
> fast as a hare
>
> handy as a hammer
>
> clear as a bright day
>
> coarse as granite
>
> so sad I could run away from home
>
> big as the sun

Few of the cliché expressions vary from this sim form, and the examples which come readily to childre will usually be almost unvarying in format. If more ideas are to be expressed, such as the notion that s

like white frosting on mountaintops, results can be obtained that frequently are of surprising excellence at all grade levels.

One of the best places to start with younger children is in the realm of nature. Young children often express themselves in similes or metaphors which involve personification.

> The thunder is a giant in the sky, beating on a drum.
>
> Snow is white cotton candy if you are only looking at it.
>
> When I look at the wind blowing on my uncle's hayfield when it is long, just before it is cut, I think of an invisible hand petting my collie dog's fur.
>
> My lizard is like he has physical fitness time every morning. He does push-ups.

> It was a gloomy night, with gray and black fog. The foghorn I could hear in the distance. Everything was very quiet except the usual creaking of the ship, and a little tugboat still tooting. There were hardly any waves. The seaweed looked like fingers of a hypnotist. Everything was still. Then the waves went crashing in. My boat was rocking steadily. Then all was quiet and still.
>
> *Mike*, grade 4

Children at all grade levels can be encouraged to appreciate the many and varied similes and metaphors found in poetry and other literature, and then led to create their own.

A sixth grade girl, when first acquainted with metaphor, told her teacher:

> "I said a metaphor this morning. I looked out the window at our fig tree which was just putting out leaves and said, 'Those aren't leaves, they are tiny green butterflies perched on all the branches.'"

As interested as children usually are in simile and metaphor, it is usually not too productive to work with these tools in isolation very far beyond the point where all the children understand the idea. These, like the other tools discussed in this chapter, should be kept ready to be used in conjunction with various writing projects as the school year progresses.

Unlike simile, metaphor, and comparison, the use of analogy lends itself well to more complete writing projects. The use of analogy—describing one thing in terms of another—requires some background on the part of the children, and therefore, better results are often obtained with older children. The sound of a bulldozer, for example, can be described in terms of a symphony orchestra, or a formal social event in terms of a football game, or unruly children running in the hallways can be likened to a flash flood in a dry wash.

Provided the group is mature enough, fables or parables may also be discussed as a method of getting across an idea. (This provides an opportunity for an introduction of the Bible as literature.) As with all the tools of the writer's trade, the use of analogy, fables, and parables should be preceded by the presentation of a good variety of examples.

How to Get Out of a Slump

Everything goes back to this general aim: to make students more effective as human beings.

Karin DeLong

So far in this book we have tried to share with you our enthusiasm for having children write and have done our best to encourage you to launch your classes on a wide variety of writing projects. We are optimistic about the successes you will have, but not unrealistic. We know that sooner or later a writing project you have launched with great expectations and which the children have begun with enthusiasm and high hopes will sag in the middle. The whole thing will suddenly seem to be getting nowhere. You may, if you wish, retreat into the teachers' room to think dark thoughts. However, having gotten you started, we shall not retreat and leave you to your own devices. Even the best of writing projects can go wrong in a number of ways. Once the problem has been defined, though, it can usually be remedied.

Unsagging a Writing Lag

One of the difficulties most often encountered is the discovery of a considerable difference between what is hoped for and what is actually accomplished. Sometimes this is apparent only to the teacher, but more often it is felt by the children, too, particularly the ones with greatest capabilities. High hopes have been held at the beginning, but when the actual job of writing is undertaken, a pall of discouragement settles in with the realization that what has actually been produced does not measure up to the original expectations.

First, by way of consolation, let us point out that this feeling is by no means unique. It occurs to even the best of adult writers, and it occurs often. In the words of Thomas Mann, "Literature is not a calling, it is a curse, believe me!"

Now that you have been consoled, what action do you take? There are several answers to this question. Perhaps you will find one in the other sections of this chapter. If you do not, perhaps a change of attitude is the answer. If your dissatisfaction with the *product* of the writing lesson is not shared by the children, then you would probably be wisest not to share it with them. Instead, the focus of your attention and theirs should be on what has been learned in the writing *process*.

If the children, too, are discouraged, the focus should remain the same. There is no reason children cannot understand that even the most famous writers face discouragement, and sometimes even desperation, over the quality of what they have produced as compared with their aspirations. Then, too, children are beginners. If they are perceptive enough to be sensitive to the flaws in their writing products, they can also perceive that what they have accomplished is beginners' work. They can be reminded that what has been accomplished in their first attempts, flawed though it may be, represents an increase over their previous writing ability, and that progress—however small it may be in terms of the finished product—has been made and can be carried over into subsequent writing projects.

More Help in Getting Writing Started

Sometimes your difficulties may have started with the beginning of your writing project. We have detailed in Chapter 2 the components of a classroom environment helpful to expression, including the providing of plenty of "input"; you may want to review these. Perhaps, though, children are having trouble with ideas about which to write because the input has not really been plentiful, has not been related enough to previous experiences, or has been too much of one kind and too little of another. In addition, perhaps the relationship of the input to the attempted writing has not been clearly shown. How would you have felt if one of your college English teachers had asked you to write an essay in tridit style on the validity of motivation of characters in Benjamin Blunkhoover's plays? You and your fellow students would have been completely stumped, having no explanation of tridit style and never having read a Blunkhoover play.

Children ordinarily produce little if they must draw upon their own experiences when their attention has not been directed toward any particular type of experience, i.e., if they must begin writing in "tridit" style, with no help in the way of explanation or experience with other writing which is similar. Then, even after some children understand what they are being asked to do, others have not yet been brought out of the dark. Explanations and suggestions from classmates can be invaluable here and should be shared with the entire class.

So, to begin with, make sure the children will have something to use in the way of content—that they have "read Blunkhoover's plays." If the topic is Halloween, bring pictures. Let the children tell out loud of some of their own Halloween experiences. If they are to write a story, for example, with a surprise ending, be sure they are acquainted with this form, which to them may be "tridit" style. Read or tell a few brief stories— about Halloween or not—which have surprise endings, or call their attention to stories with surprise endings which they have already experienced in their readers or elsewhere.

Once the "input" for a specific writing assignment has been taken care of for both form and content, the job is still not done. Children, particularly those who are less mature, need help with the basic components of putting ideas into writing, i.e., with words. If the topic is Halloween, the children can suggest word lists in various categories, which the teacher can list for all to see as the story work progresses. How do children feel on Halloween? A word list to answer this question might include *excited, scared, spooky, frightened, happy, goosebumpy,* and so on. There is no harm in a teacher's providing some of the words when the children's inspiration begins to flag. Then, what kinds of costumes do children wear? Skeleton, witch, clown, cat, Indian, robot, and so forth can be provided, along with all the additional listings which might be appropriate to the story assignment. Putting the lists on large sheets of paper is preferable to using the chalkboard, so that they can quickly be taken down and replaced if the project is carried over more than one time period. In this way, children are not constantly raising their hands to know how to spell a word, and they may scan the lists for ideas when they need them. Word lists should not be limited to nouns. Verbs and adverbs and adjectives are just as helpful when listed for reference.

Some children need help in making their writing ideas specific enough. Ask thirty pupils to write a story about a dog, and a few of them are ready to start. Those who are not need to be asked, What does the dog in your story look like? Is he large? What color is he? Is he just a puppy? Is his tail long or short? Is he friendly to everybody, or does he like to be petted only by his master? Who is his master? Does he sleep in a doghouse or with the family? Are you going to write about the tricks he can do? Would you rather just tell about what he did in one hour's time? Would you like to tell what this dog would do if he were taken for an outing at the beach?

Probably even after this much help, there will be some children still at a loss as to where to start. This may be the time to ask various children to give the opening sentence or sentences of their story. With some classes, or assignments, it may work out better to have the entire class write the opening of a story. And if this proves difficult, it may really show that the assignment is too much for the class to handle as individuals and the entire project should be completed as a group endeavor. If only a small portion of the class cannot handle the story writing, they may write a group story with the assistance of the teacher while the remainder of the class work as individuals. Another useful arrangement is to have some of the children work in pairs or trios, with ideas from each and help in getting them on paper from the most able.

Extra Help As They Write

Once children have been given an extra boost in starting writing, subsequent difficulties in the way of "I can't finish this because I don't know what to do" frequently are eliminated, or at least greatly reduced. The largest single area of difficulty remaining seems to be with narratives which cannot be "wound up." Often this is because a child continues expanding his narration, involving more and more characters and turns of plot, until all of his writing energy is expended. He then either slaps on a sentence such as "And then they all went home," or just plain gives up. Usually an ounce of prevention is the best of cures. Particularly if the writing project is some sort of narrative, the teacher should take pains to make sure that *all* of the children understand the need to limit the scope of their project. Only so many characters, so large an area, so long a time scope can be presented in any one writing project, even if it be a trilogy of historical novels.

Any writer simply has better results when he limits the framework of his task. A science story about spiders can run to three or four pages of generalized and none too interesting information about arachnids. Three pages on the feeding habits of black widow spiders can be much more interesting and a great deal easier to organize and write.

A little "group therapy" is also often an excellent help. Perhaps about the time the first child comes to you with a "What shall I do now?" query, you should ask the class to stop and listen to the story. Why limit the child to the help of your ideas only, when the mental resources of the entire class are available? The reading of a few more partly-finished projects can be a two-way help—both to find answers to the problems of the children whose stories are read and to provide additional ideas for the listeners. Help may also be secured, if the entire class has problems of this sort, by taking a few of the stories which may particularly merit further attention and allotting individual children further time to work on them, or by working as a class to polish an ending just to see what can be done with it. In many cases, however, it may be best simply to call a halt to the project, with the realization that you and the children have not attained what was sought. This is not to say that little has been accomplished, however, and this is an important point to be gotten across to children. Undoubtedly much will have been learned in the writing attempt, and the majority of the classes will quickly realize this once it is pointed out; in fact, the children will probably take a great deal of satisfaction in pointing out the many things which have been learned.

Christopher Columbus

REPORTER: "What is your name?"

COLUMBUS: "My name is Christopher Columbus and I just discovered America."

REPORTER: "Tell me about your big voyage to America."

COLUMBUS: "I volunteered to go to America. We had been traveling for two weeks and not a sign of land. They started to betray me but I fought them with my sword."

REPORTER: "Go on! Go on!"

COLUMBUS: "After three months of traveling the food supplies ran out. The crew and I were getting hungry. One of the men was going to kill me when a man in the crow's nest yelled 'Land Ahoy!' Everybody went to shore. When I looked at my chart, I saw that we were on an uncharted island. We looked over the island to see if there was anybody there. There wasn't. We went to sleep."

REPORTER: "Then what did you do?"

COLUMBUS: "When we awoke we were ready to go home. When we got home I went to see the Queen of Spain and told her what had happened and we discovered America. She gave us a medal."

REPORTER: "Thank you for the information, Chris."

Mary, grade 6

A Word on Rewriting

Rewriting stories, compositions, and the like because they are not "neat," or because of errors in spelling and so forth, is a laborious task for some children and, if always required, a distasteful one. Sometimes it is just better to start over than to rewrite, as most adults have found out at some time in their lives. Actually, the only writing that should be rewritten is that which is basically good but needs "touching up."

For necessary rewriting, the first thing you will have to do is give the children a reason for wanting to go back over their "completed" work. You may find that there isn't a reason, short of a messy-appearing page, a misplaced comma, or a misspelled word. If you feel that rewriting in such an instance must be done, why not let the recopying wait and count it later as a handwriting practice session?

When there are reasons for reworking the writing, the children should be helped to see them. Hearing their stories read aloud (with plenty of praise for the good parts) or coming back to them at a later date may be enough. Perhaps it will be helpful to have the group make suggestions to revise one story (pick a young author with enough self-confidence). Some helpful changes will be self-evident. For further improvements the previous writing instruction given to the class can be reviewed as a checklist. Use of direct quotes, alliteration, better verbs, more explicit metaphors, etc., can be gone over.

In addition, it is sometimes wise to consider the following for suggesting to the children:

1. Transformation: changing from passive to active, declarative to interrogative, interchanging clauses, etc.
2. Relocation: changing the order of thoughts presented, changing the linear order of sentences, using an element from the beginning in the ending.
3. Elimination: getting rid of extraneous or irrelevant matter.
4. Expansion: getting across an idea by illustration, amplification, emphasis, and sometimes even repetition.

And don't be afraid to help and suggest—you're getting paid to teach—but do it on the spot, with the child as the active partner.

What Have You Wrought?

. . . when we have something to say and the words are on the tip of our pens to say it, what power we unleash!

Mauree Applegate

The evaluation aspect of a writing program may be a headache for you. If so, you're not alone. Most teachers have difficulties with measuring results and knowing what to do after they have been measured. Too often evaluation means giving a grade on a paper, or, after a period of time, reporting a grade on a card for the writing done during a time period. These things bring about most teachers' consternation and annoyance. As evaluation is thought of only in relation to grades, there is certain to be reaction in the writing program that will not be productive of effective expression or creativity. All teachers really know this down deep, but so frequently they allow a general concern with grades, an insistence upon comparison of one pupil with another to persist while, at the same time, they try to puzzle out why their pupils aren't more creative, why student writing is drab, and why there seems to be so little improvement.

Evaluation is, of course, more than mere grades; it is more than just comparing one pupil or his achievements with others or simply marking on a pupil's paper. In a writing program evaluation should include appraising the program itself and the teaching procedures and materials used. It should also include measuring the general quality of writing and that of each pupil, and assessing pupils' growth during particular time lapses and from one writing activity to another.

Comparisons which handicap a writing program do not have to be made. Papers need not be marked with symbols indicating deficiencies. The end does not have to be the assigning of grades. Teachers simply must reject an obsequiousness to public and administrative demands to make all teaching result in grades, which are essentially nothing but letters of the alphabet or numerals, and are, in addition, comparisons among things that are not comparable. Authority does not have to be flaunted, nor public concern ignored. What is needed is simply that teachers know their objectives and, thus, what they are evaluating and for what purpose. The intent here is to focus upon what should be evaluated in writing and why, to help teachers gain the professional knowledge needed or to reinforce what they already know, so that they may stand pat on a sensible program of evaluation.

Goals and Evaluation

Joseph Conrad once defined his writing goals as "To make you feel; to make you hear; to make you touch; to make you see—." Large goals, surely, are perhaps possible of achievement only by a skilled and honest observer and writer, but are also goals to be sought by even a beginning writer. It is in terms of such goals that we should think as we evaluate.

Essentially a writer is seeking to communicate—an idea, a thought, a feeling, a piece of information, or a point of view (Conrad's goals expressed another way). No writer sets as his goal the writing of "correct" English, or the inclusion of someone's notion of the proper amount of punctuation, or the introduction of each paragraph with a topic sentence. Yet how often is children's writing evaluated in these terms!

Certainly punctuation, acceptable usage, and good paragraph construction may facilitate the communication of ideas and feelings, but taken separately or all together these are mechanical elements and skills or reflections of an environment; they are not, in any case, the most important parts of writing. Every teacher really knows this and simply needs to take stock of his evaluation procedures and give proper recognition to this knowledge

Knowledge of the objectives of instruction are basic to an evaluation of that instruction. Obviously a writing program has more than a single objective or goal, and all such goals must be considered in an evaluation. But they do not have to be considered of equal importance, nor must we place greatest emphasis upon those goals which may be easiest to evaluate. Surely it is easier to determine whether a child has learned to set off an appositive by commas than it is to asssess his understanding of how to organize an idea for most effective communication to a reader. The multiple goals of a writing program need to be placed in a hierarchical arrangement—different perhaps for each evaluative purpose and for different pupils, but giving proper recognition to those things which are the true goals of the writing program.

Evaluating the Program

Before looking at children's writing efforts and the products of these efforts and how they may be evaluated, let us consider the evaluation of a teaching program. Such evaluation raises questions, questions which do not have simple and/or single answers. Actually, each teacher must ask his own questions, for each is an individual and is working with children who are individuals. Each teacher must also answer his own questions. There are no set questions and no "right" answers. There are guidelines to an effective writing program and many suggestions for instruction, and both have received attention in the preceding pages. These need to be considered as a teacher formulates his questions and gives his answers. Above all, it is important to ask questions which really focus upon the program and to give answers that are really truthful. The goal of a teacher in evaluating a writing program is to improve that program; no other goal is defensible.

What are you seeking in your teaching of writing? Are you seeking products, or are you teaching a process? Are the products those things the children have put on paper, or are they various elements of the children's growth? Is the process you teach that of putting words together into sentences and paragraphs, or is it that of a child giving expression and helping to fulfill himself as a person?

These are not easy questions to answer. The good teacher surely is most interested in helping each child grow as much as possible. But growth is usually measured in performance and the written product is evidence of performance. Certainly teachers must be concerned with the written product and how acceptable it is as communication. They must also be concerned with how this product came about. What processes has a child developed that permitted him to create this product?

We need generally to ask, What is the writing program doing to and for the children—and each child—in the class? Isn't, then, the child the chief product and his growth the chief process?

As suggested above, perhaps the answers to such questions may be derived from a consideration of the writing products. Is the writing generally vapid and superficial and trite? Does it neither interest nor communicate? Surely children are not this way. They are eager and sad, exhilarated and frustrated, interested and bored, possessing and giving. If you say their writing fails to express these feelings, if it is stale and unimaginative, then something has surely happened. Something in your writing program (or in that of teachers before you) has come between them and the papers they turn in to you. You need to examine (evaluate) your program!

Some things that might have caused the children's papers to be something less than you had desired and hoped for are the following, and you can add to this list with a bit of thought:

1. Lack of direction and guidance.
2. Fear of teacher disapproval.
3. Stifled oral expression.
4. A meager vocabulary.
5. Ignorance of the forms of writing.
6. A deficiency of input.
7. Failure to recognize the importance of the audience.

8. No working knowledge of composition skills.
9. Killing ideas by putting paper before the children too soon.
10. A drudgery approach to punctuation teaching.

As you think about your writing program, try to think in specific ways. Think of what you are trying to accomplish, not with some hypothetical class or with some class that you wish you had, but with the class that you are teaching, with each child in that class. Then remember that what works for one teacher with one group of children may not work for another teacher and another group of children. Evaluate your program, yes, but do it sensibly and thoughtfully.

Evaluating Children's Writing

The kind of evaluation we seek is essentially a matter of self-appraisal. Whether it is a teacher asking and answering questions about his program of instruction, or a child looking at his most recently written story or his letter of thanks to the supermarket manager for the class's tour, the fundamental question is one of self-appraisal.

Admittedly it may not be easy to get the children in your class to evaluate their writing, but it is likely that this is one result of the writing program they have experienced. It is simply a concern of every human being to appraise what he has done and, if a child does not do this for his own writing, it is because he fears the teacher's reaction—a reaction which his experience tells him will be negative and fault-finding. As a defense mechanism he feigns his unconcern. Often this mechanism has been developed to such a degree—his writing assignments have been so routine and so far removed from his interests and needs—that he is actually unaware of his resistance to appraising his work. When children have been engaged in expression that to them is purposeful, they are interested in evaluating their efforts. Only as they are allowed to grow are they concerned with knowing that they are growing. And as they know they are growing, they receive the stimulation which success brings and they have the inner motivation to seek new opportunities for expression.

From the beginning of instruction in written expression pupils should be encouraged to depend upon themselves in making their writing show their best efforts. They should learn to examine carefully what they have written in terms of selection of the thought or idea; organization, clarity, and appeal of the product; and courtesy shown to their readers by legibility, correct spelling, acceptable word usage, and meaningful punctuation. This does not mean that everything a child writes needs to be given this kind of scrutiny; not every product is written for an audience, nor is all writing done for a well-defined purpose. Children sometimes write just to be writing, as all of us do to some extent and at some times. But when the child writes to communicate and to express, as all children will unless their desire for expression is shut off or no opportunities exist, whether it be a story, a poem, a report, or a letter, he should appraise what he has written.

Standards

One good way to help children learn to appraise or evaluate their writing is through the use of standards with which to compare their writing. These standards, or rules, or lists of things to remember should be developed by the children themselves and should not be fixed but should be evolving from one writing experience to another. The standards should be reasonably possible of attainment by the children and in each case should be developed from examination of deficiencies in previous writing attempts. Focus should be upon such things as, Have I said what I wanted to say? Is my story well organized? Do I have a good beginning and a good ending? but may also include, Have I begun each sentence with a capital letter? Are all the words spelled correctly?

One Class's Standards

Our Story Formula

1. Does my story have a good beginning?
2. Does my story show a reader what the story idea is?

3. Does my story reach a high point or climax?
4. Do all parts of the story fit together?

A Proofreading Chart

Proofreading My Story

1. Is my paper headed correctly?
2. Did I skip a line after my heading?
3. Did I capitalize the important words in my title?
4. Did I skip a line before I began to write my story?
5. Did I indent for each paragraph?
6. Do I have margins?
7. Is each word spelled correctly?
8. Have I used good sentences?
9. Did I use the correct punctuation?
10. Did I include important points in my story?
11. Did I tell my story in sequence?
12. Did I use new and interesting words?

Standards may be developed for a class or for a group within a class, but each child may also be helped to develop his own standards, since group standards may be so general that they fail to take into account the different abilities of the children. On the other hand, the general nature of group standards may be enough for all or most of the children to evaluate their writing by and yet will allow each child to avoid a comparison of his writing with that of other children. Another approach which may better do this is to word the standards so that the statements relate to each child's writing. For example, Is this story better than my last one? How many new words did I use in this story? or, more specifically, Is my story told in good order? and Is each sentence a good sentence?

Standards cannot be the same for all kinds of writing. Poetry and letter writing are not judged in the same manner and children should learn this. True, some, or perhaps most, mechanical elements—punctuation, margins, etc.—can be the same or nearly so, but standards for appraisal of content must be different. The children can readily sense this and will themselves state the things for a particular kind of writing that should be observed.

Proofreading

Simple proofreading skills should be taught when children first begin to write. In these early stages the standards which the teacher and children have developed may serve as a guide for the proofreading. As children progress through the grades, however, they should be encouraged to develop for themselves criteria for observance in proofreading. These criteria should have a different focus from the standards used in evaluation as suggested previously but they are no less a part of the self-evaluation process.

It is not enough for a teacher to say, "Proofread what you have written"—an admonition meaningless to young children and ineffective for older ones without instruction in how proofreading is done. The steps in the total proofreading process should be taught one at a time. That is, at first children may be asked to see if each sentence begins with a capital letter. When this has been learned, move on to a second step, such as, Are all your words spelled correctly? Are there any you want to ask about? This process may be continued and the number of things to look for extended as needed. For some children this extension may be more rapid than for others. Do not have children try to do proofreading beyond that which they can do effectively and with meaning to themselves.

Lessons in proofreading may be given by having children check a duplicated paragraph that contains errors. Also, try having a committee of proofreaders (three students, but alternating ones) do proofreading for a writing project. When they finish their work they may place it in a box called "rewrite." Children may be shown the value of proofreading by displaying work labeled "Before proofreading" and "After proofreading." Oral reading of a child's writing is a good way to cause him to notice that something doesn't sound right or make sense. Particularly will he note omitted words, incomplete statements, and faulty punctuation.

Models

Models can be used as a form of standards for guiding evaluation. Models of letters, written reports, and other written products that tend to be somewhat standardized in form are found in textbooks and may be used by the children to compare with their own writing. Another good way is to have a child write a letter or report, getting it in the very best form possible, and then use it as his model for future endeavors with this particular form of writing.

It is more difficult to use models for judging poetry and stories. Sometimes a teacher may write a story developed in such a way as to focus upon particular things he is trying to teach to the children and may use this as a model. For example, such a story might have a good beginning and build up to a climax near the end. Or perhaps it contains particularly good verbs if the teacher wants to help children get away from some of the overworked ones. Professional writing may also be used as models.

There is some danger in an excessive use of models since there may be a tendency to make writing like that of the model. This is not the purpose of the model, of course, and if this tendency develops, models should be discarded and greater emphasis given to drawing out individual ideas and thoughts, with less regard to their organization and form.

The same may be true for standards. It all depends upon how the emphasis is given. If the children are given the freedom to decide for themselves how the models and standards will be used and then allowed to use them themselves for genuine self-evaluation, the possibility of a problem of inhibiting creativeness and expression should be minimized.

A Final Word

We are not so foolish that we fail to recognize that you and your fellow teachers must put symbols on report cards but we assert that this task need not get the upper hand. The teacher who must put grades on cards should do so in a professional manner, considering the goals he has set, what he has attempted to do, and the needs of each child.

Grades given should not be the climax of a fault-finding approach to evaluating children's writing. Rather they should result from using the red pencil to show the good idea, the colorful phrase, the active verb, the effective organization of thought. This procedure will make the grade-giving a more positively oriented, easier, and more professional task.

We recognize that with all that has been said you may feel that you have accomplished little and that the children write no more effectively than before your efforts began. We urge, though, that you take the longer view—look at the children's writing after two or three years' efforts by you and your colleagues and we are sure you will discover you have wrought something very fine indeed.

More Aids

A Writing Lesson Based Upon
a Literature Selection

Objective: To have pupils write a short selection which gives attention to details and creates a feeling.

Procedure: Duplicate the following passage for distribution. Have the pupils read the selection silently, and have one pupil read it aloud. Give attention as necessary to unfamiliar words.

From *On the Banks of Plum Creek*

Soon after Ma came back from the stable, the frost on the eastern window glowed faintly yellow. Laura ran to breathe on it and scratch away the ice until she made a peep-hole. Outdoors the sun was shining!

Ma looked out, then Mary and Laura took turns looking out at the snow blowing in waves over the ground. The sky looked like ice. Even the air looked cold about that fast-blowing flood of snow, and the sunshine that came through the peep-hole was no warmer than a shadow.

Laura Ingalls Wilder

Discussion: Ask questions of the pupils based upon this selection. For example, some to ask might include these:

1. What kind of day is it? How do you know?
2. Where had Ma been? What might she have been doing? How do you suppose she was dressed?
3. Why did the frost glow on the eastern window? Do you suppose the house was cold?
4. How does snow blow in waves?
5. How does ice look?
6. Why did the author say "flood of snow"? Can you "see" a flood of snow?
7. What other words could you use to describe a windy, snow-covered scene?
8. Who do you suppose Mary and Laura were? What do you think they might do on this cold day? Where do you think they lived?

Continue the discussion, directing it at eliciting settings for stories related to their classroom or any other setting familiar to all the children in which a feeling arises from the physical surroundings. For example, questions might be directed at the current day:

1. Does it look warm outside? Why do you say it does?
2. Is the sun shining? Can you see anything that might show you how hot the sun feels?
3. What are the things you see which indicate to you the season of the year? Name as many as you can.
4. What sounds can be heard? Which are pleasant? Unpleasant?
5. How many things in our scene are in motion?
6. Select one particular small area in the scene. Describe it as carefully as you can.

During this discussion, note in writing for the class the words and phrases which would be useful in writing a description of the scene. Emphasis should be given to those which are particularly apt or original.

After this preparation the class will be ready to construct together the opening paragraphs of a story. It should be easier to write this in an interesting style if there are one or more persons in the scene, doing something and reacting to the surroundings. Perhaps a child and a small dog who has wandered onto the school ground might be included. Take every opportunity for improving the wording as children suggest sentences.

Here is one group product from this procedure:

Joey came around the corner of the old brick school building, scuffling his feet in the dead leaves which had blown onto the walkway. Although the sunlight was bright enough to make him squint his eyes, the day was cold. Behind him the small dog followed in a zig-zagging way, moving from one pile of leaves to another whenever the leaves were stirred by the slight breeze.

A Class Newspaper

Opportunity for much writing can occur through the production of a class newspaper. The writing may be of many types since newspapers ordinarily include many things—news stories, special features, letters to the editor, jokes, advertisements, poems, and comics.

When organizing a newspaper project, the teacher should keep flexibility in mind. This can be a minimum or a maximum project; there is a great variety of possible temporary or permanent forms it can take.

The best start might be a unit on newspapers. As learning progresses, class enthusiasm and practical limitations can help determine how far and in what direction the project will go. (Pitfall: Avoid definite statements at the start as to how often the paper will come out, or that it will be permanent.)

Possible "outlets" for newspaper work: a room or school newspaper or news sheet (published either regularly or irregularly), contributions to P.T.A. newsletter, to a small local paper or "shopping news." (Many such publications have difficulty getting enough local material and would welcome such contributions.)

The Newspaper Unit

Many upper-grade reading programs include material on how to read a newspaper. This provides a good starting point. Children might read newspapers together in class and analyze them, bringing clippings of various sorts to illustrate what they learn. Various sections of a paper (sports, society news, etc.) should be noted. Children should become aware of types of news stories—local, international, human interest, and so forth. Special attention should be given to sources of newspaper material—syndicated, wire services, publicity handouts, and local reporting. Journalism has its own vocabulary, and children may learn the special meanings of words such as copy, deadline, proofreading, layout, and editor.

The Newspaper Corner

This is worthwhile even if the class is only playing at journalism for a short time or making contributions to other news sheets. It should include a place to keep clippings and samples of other publications, special work materials (including a typewriter if at all possible), a display file of completed work, and working space.

Actual Newspaper Writing

To get started, it is usually helpful to do the following:

(1) Prepare appropriate version of a staff diagram. Discuss it with the class, then mount it on the wall near the newspaper corner. Under each title thumbtack the name of the person filling the job along with a statement of exact duties. Fill positions starting at top. If an entire class is not participating, any jobholder may fill vacant posts under him. Positions should be assigned on the basis of ability rather than popularity.

(2) Have try-outs; assign all posts temporarily.

(3) Have the class work up lists of "runs" (news sources to visit regularly), and suggest trial deadlines for copy.

(4) Set up a datebook with dates of coming news events and ideas for assignments.

Writing Style

Avoid "journalese" and urge simple, direct language, with the most important items first. Go over the basics: who, what, when, where, why; the "pyramid" story. Stress accuracy of facts and reliability of sources. Standard editing and proofreading marks may be introduced if desired.

A Typical Newspaper Staff

Executive editor: Is responsible for the entire operation—in most situations this position would be combined with that of business manager.

Business manager: Supervises activities of the circulation manager and the auditor, plus any activities which are "business" rather than "editorial."

Circulation manager: Distributes copies of the paper and keeps record of those outside of classroom receiving copies.

Auditor: Is in charge of keeping all financial records.

Managing editor: Directs the entire editorial staff. May do little writing or editing, but supplies ideas.

News editor: Lays out work, keeps datebook, and keeps track of copy in process of writing.

Reporters: Gather news.

Staff writers: Write articles (if reporters do not write their own articles).

Makeup editor: Keeps track of completed copy and proof (if any), makes up paper and directs copy editors.

Copy editors: Do headline writing, copyreading, and proofreading.

Department editor: Delivers material from departments to makeup editor, and keeps track of their copy that is in process of being written. May assist sports and social editors in keeping of their own datebooks.

Art editor: Directs or is artist, or photographer if method of duplicating paper permits. May judge or appoint judges for artwork submitted for publication. Delivers material to makeup editor.

Bibliographies

Books for Your Children

. . . to help them sharpen their senses of hearing, sight, smell, touch, and taste.

Borten, Helen, *Do You Hear What I Hear?* London, Abelard-Schuman, 1960.

Borten, Helen, *Do You See What I See?* London, Abelard-Schuman, 1959.

Elkin, Benjamin, *The Loudest Noise in the World.* New York, Viking, 1954.

Emberley, Ed, *The Wing of a Flea.* Boston, Little, Brown, 1961.

Fisher, Aileen, *Going Barefoot.* New York, Crowell, 1960.

Liberty, Gene, *The First Book of the Human Senses.* New York, F. Watts, 1961.

Marks, Marcia, *Swing Me, Swing Tree.* Boston, Little, Brown, 1959.

McGrath, Thomas, *The Beautiful Things.* New York, Vanguard, 1960.

O'Neill, Mary, *Hailstones and Halibut Bones.* New York, Doubleday, 1961.

Schwartz, J., *Through the Magnifying Glass.* New York, Whittlesey, 1954.

Showers, Paul, *Find Out by Touching.* New York, Crowell, 1961.

Showers, Paul, *The Listening Walk.* New York, Crowell, 1961.

Spooner, Jane, *Tony Plays with Sounds*. New York, John Day, 1961.
Webber, Irma E., *It Looks Like This*. New York, Scott, 1958.

. . . to help them respond and identify emotionally with other objects, people, or situations.

Boxer, Devorah, *26 Ways to Be Somebody Else*. New York, Pantheon, 1960.
Brown, Margaret Wise, *The Dead Bird*. New York, Scott, 1958.
Buckley, Peter, *Jan of Holland*. New York, F. Watts, 1956.
Charlip, Remy, *Where Is Everybody?* Eau Claire, Wisc., E. M. Hale, n.d.
Conger, Marion, *Who Has Seen the Wind?* New York, Abingdon, 1959.
Crowell, Pers, *What Can a Horse Do That You Can't Do?* New York, McGraw-Hill, 1954.
Fenton, Edward, *Fierce John*. New York, Doubleday, 1959.
Huntington, Harriett, *Let's Go Outdoors*. New York, Doubleday, 1939.
Icenhower, Joseph B., *Antarctic*. New York, F. Watts, 1956.
Krauss, Ruth, and Johnson, Crockett, *Is This You?* New York, Harper & Row, 1955.
Lenski, Lois, *Now It's Fall*. New York, Oxford, 1948.
Lionni, Leo, *Little Blue and Little Yellow*. New York, Obolensky, 1959.
Livingston, Myra Cohn, *Whispers and Other Poems*. New York, Harcourt, Brace & World, 1958.
Radlauer, Ruth S., *Of Course, You're a Horse*. New York, Abelard-Schuman, 1959.
Rounds, Glen, *Wildlife at Your Doorstep*. Englewood Cliffs, New Jersey, Prentice-Hall, 1958.
Schultz, Charles, *Happiness Is a Warm Puppy*. San Francisco, Determined Productions, 1962.
Tresselt, Alvin R., *White Snow, Bright Snow*. New York, Lothrop, 1947.
Varley, Dimitry, *The Whirly Bird*. New York, Knopf, 1961.
Yates, Elizabeth, *A Place for Peter*. New York, Coward-McCann, 1952.

. . . to help them become sensitized to one object, exploring it from many viewpoints.

Bartlett, Margaret, *The Clean Brook*. New York, Crowell, 1960.

Belting, Natalia, *The Sun Is a Golden Earring*. New York, Holt, Rinehart and Winston, 1962.

Conklin, Gladys, *I Like Butterflies*. New York, Holiday, 1960.

Conklin, Gladys, and Latham, B., *I Like Caterpillars*. New York, Holiday, 1958.

de Regniers, Beatrice, *The Shadow Book*. New York, Harcourt, Brace
& World, 1960.

Gordon, Isabel, *The ABC Hunt*. New York, Viking, 1961.

Huntington, Harriet, *Let's Go Outdoors*. New York, Doubleday, 1939.

Mace, Katherine, *A Tail Is a Tail*. New York, Abelard-Schuman, 1961.

Paschel, Herbert, *The First Book of Color*. New York, F. Watts, 1959.

Rood, Ronald, *The How and Why Wonder Book of Insects*. New York,
Grosset & Dunlap, 1960.

Shuttlesworth, Dorothy, *The Story of Spiders*. New York, Garden
City, 1959.

Udry, Janice May, *A Tree Is Nice*. New York, Harper & Row, 1956.

Williamson, Margaret, *The First Book of Bugs*. Toronto, Ambassador
Books, Ltd., 1960.

Zim, Herbert S., *Goldfish*. New York, Morrow, 1947.

. . . let them look at these, too.

Fitzhugh, Louise, *Harriet the Spy*. New York, Harper & Row, 1964.

Treanor, John H., *A First Thesaurus*. Cambridge, Mass., Educators
Publishing Service, 1963.

Yates, Elizabeth, *Someday You'll Write*. New York, Dutton, 1962.

And to Stimulate You Further

Applegate, Mauree, *Freeing Children to Write*. New York, Harper &
Row, 1963.

Applegate, Mauree, *Winged Words*. New York, Harper & Row,
1961.

Arnstein, Flora J., *Adventure into Poetry*. Stanford, Stanford University Press, 1951.

Barbe, Walter, "Creative Writing Activities," in *Highlights Handbook*.
Columbus, Ohio, Highlights for Children, Inc., 1965.

Burrows, Alvina Treut, and others, "Children's Writing: Research in

Composition and Related Skills." *Elementary English,* Vol. 36, No. 2 (February, 1959), pp. 106-121.

Burrows, Alvina Treut, and others, *They All Want to Write.* New York, Prentice-Hall, 1952.

Carlson, Ruth Kearney, "Developing An Original Person." *Elementary English,* Vol. 41, No. 3 (March, 1964), pp. 268-292.

Carlson, Ruth Kearney, "Seventeen Qualities of Creative Writing." *Elementary English,* Vol. 28, No. 8 (December, 1961), pp. 576-579.

Carlson, Ruth Kearney, *Sparkling Words: Two Hundred Practical and Creative Writing Ideas.* Hayward, Calif., Cal-State Bookstore, 1965.

Fantani, Mario D., "Open Versus Closed Classrooms." *The Clearing House,* Vol. 37, No. 2 (October, 1962), pp. 67-71.

Greene, Harry A., and Petty, Walter T., *Developing Language Skills in the Elementary Schools,* 2nd ed. Boston, Allyn and Bacon, 1963, Chap. 13.

Marksberry, Mary Lee, *Foundation of Creativity.* New York, Harper & Row, 1963.

Myers, R. E., and Torrance, E. Paul, "Can Teachers Encourage Creative Thinking?" *Educational Leadership,* Vol. 19, No. 3 (December, 1961), pp. 156-59.

Torrance, E. Paul, *Education and the Creative Potential.* Minneapolis, University of Minnesota Press, 1963.

Trauger, Wilmer K., "Language," in *Language Arts in Elementary Schools.* New York, McGraw-Hill, 1963.

Walter, Nina Wallis, *Let Them Write Poetry.* New York, Holt, Rinehart and Winston, 1962.

Zirbes, Laura, "A Creative Conception of the Language Arts in the Curriculum," in *Spurs to Creative Teaching.* New York, Putnam, 1959.